To: Debbie,

Hope you ~~put~~ don't

Put the Fire Out...

in your Pants!

Chuck

CONTENTS

Acknowledgements

The author (me) would like to thank both the Highlands 20 and Eastern Nevada Interagency Fire for employing him and giving him the fodder to write this book. And a special 'thank you' to all the men and women I met and made friends with during my time as a wildland firefighter, the memories we made – both the good and the bad. In fact, I owe this whole book to them.

I am also beholden to the men and women in all areas of wildland firefighting and the countless sacrifices they make each and every fire season, for without them our country would not be the same.

To honor all wildland firefighters, especially those who have lost their lives on the job, I will be donating 10% of all books sold to the Wildland Firefighter Foundation (wffoundation.org) who unceasingly help those who have given their lives for the greater good.

I also owe a huge debt of gratitude to the insanely gorgeous and extremely talented Rebecca Hoyle for reading, scrutinizing, and editing the essays in this book. Words cannot do justice to how much she helped shape each essay from its primordial stage to what you see before you today. Without her this book would be little more than frothy dribble and vague recollections.

I am also grateful to my mother and father for always believing in me and encouraging me to write my heart out, as well as to my teachers and professors Lynn Schott, Brian Golphene, Jim Krusoe, Monona Wali, Rachel Toor, and Polly Buckingham who taught me everything I know about the writing process, for without their guidance my writing would be middling at best, thank you.

Introduction

In June of 2013, on summer break from my first year of college, I started a job as a wildland firefighter with the Highlands 20, an initial attack handcrew, based out of the Sinlahekin Valley in North Central Washington. I had never before thought of fighting wildfire, but my bank account was in dire straits and, truth be told, so was my ego. However, I didn't start that summer looking for personal growth, I started it with nineteen other men, each of us looking for a seasonal gig that paid well. I was already a man and thought that I knew quite a bit about myself, about the world at large.

But as that summer, and that fire season progressed; I found out that I still had so much to learn; I was both a rookie to wildland firefighting and a rookie in life. Through the trials of day-to-day life on the fireline, living and fighting wildfire with my fire crew, through the adrenaline, the danger, the laughter, the smoke, the blisters, I came to understand that it was far more than a paycheck that I was earning. I was learning, for the first time in a long while, who I really was and what I was made of. I was proving my worth to the fire crew. I was proving my worth to myself.

This book evolved out of experiences from my four summers of fighting wildfire as well as to a promise I made to my fellow Highlands 20 crewmembers. I promised them that I would write a book about wildland fire fighting. At the time I had no idea what that would entail. But I knew what it would not. It would not be a book about hero-izing the exploits of wildland firefighters. No, bullshitting the reader with portrayals of wildland firefighters as faultless demigods with the morals of saints, the work ethic of Navy SEALs, and the looks of A-list Hollywood actors was never my intention.

I make no claim to have been a perfect wildland firefighter, or to have never felt fear when putting my life on the line in battles with Nature. I know for a fact that there are many other fire crews that saw more action and were in far greater danger than the Highlands 20 or I ever were.

This book is by no means the definitive book about wildland firefighting. That book would be impossible to write, as every person who fought wildfire has their own experiences that vary greatly from my own. What I have found is that are no two fire seasons alike. And that my time spent on the fireline was a perfect balance of danger and laughter, of bravery and childlike awe, of crassness and brotherhood, of selflessness and evolution.

State of Fire is neither an ultimate description of wildland firefighting nor a book of fire-filled heroism, so you might be asking then, what is its purpose? This is a book about wildland firefighting and the indelible marks it leaves on a person's soul. This book is about finding commonality by going through hardship with strangers, who soon become closer than family. It's about what can be learned from camaraderie, and what happens when you separate men from society and normalcy for months at a time. It's about love and loss, and the rebirth of one's self through the testing of mental, emotional, and physical strength. It is about coming to terms with one's limitations, and why challenges of every shade should not be shunned, but embraced. It is about finding meaning and worth, where once there was none. And most importantly, why these lessons were not only significant for me, but for everyone who picks up this book.

This book represents - my path to, of, and away from wildland firefighting.

It should be noted that State of Fire is a collection of nine essays. Each essay deals with a different aspect of wildland firefighting. Therefore it does not have to be read in chronological order, as each essay is independent of the next.

State of Fire

Silver Creek Fire (2014). Photo Credit: Jimmy Gonzalez

The President declares a state of emergency. It is Washington State from June through September of 2015, and it is suffering from savage wildfires where the earth burns from lack of rain and every firefighting resource within a 200 mile radius and the National Guard and the US Army and citizen volunteers and firefighters from as far away as Arkansas and New Jersey and Australia and New Zealand are called to the fight. It is a State of evacuations and looting and where a multitude of family homes go the way of the flame. Fires burst beyond containment lines. 50 mile per hour winds rip through the guts of the State. Three wildland firefighters lose their lives. It is a State that is breaking the wrong kind of record, that of destruction by wildfire. By summers end it's dubbed the "worst-ever" fire season in Washington's history, losing more than 1,000,000 acres to the ravages of Nature, and leaving a $178 million IOU for the State to cover.

There is drought upon the land, a result of too few inches of wintertime snowpack and too little rain, and the forests are sick and overgrown and dying and fire-prone, and the grasslands are infected with cheatgrass, a hot and fast burning and invasive species.

Nature has reached a breaking point and is fighting back the only way it knows how: using wildfire to butcher forests and abort humans from their habitations, and because it is my summertime profession I spend this summer like I have the previous two, as a wildland firefighter on the Highlands 20, an initial attack fire crew.

Early in the summer of 2015 the Highlands 20 makes a pit stop at a roadside gas station. This sentence is stenciled on the window.

The Best Has Just Arrived.

The words seem a good omen for us and our upcoming fire season, and not just for my fire crew but for me, because right now I feel I am the best, I'm at my apex: my spirit is high, my body is strong, my mind set on victory. I'm a decade or more older than the rest of my fire crew, but I tell myself that age is just a number and I believe it.

The fact that that slogan was used to advertise fried chicken is no longer lost on me. I might have begun that fire season feeling that I was the best, but by its end, I would be just like a piece of that advertised-heat-lamp-singed-chicken: desiccated, crusty, past my prime.

In the hot June of 2015 the Highlands 20 are at Central Washington University for ten days of fire-related classes. They are meant to sharpen our wildland firefighting savvy to a fine point with lessons related to leadership, heat related illness, and other fire related topics. What they are, however, are an exercise in futility, as each night my fire crew carouses through the town's bars and by day struggles to stay awake through ten-hour sessions of things we either already know, or that we just don't care about.

Here, amongst our fire brethren from all four corners of Washington State, the talk might be of fire and drought and weather patterns and record breaking heat and levels of destruction, but not once do I think of the danger, or my family, or the people that will be affected. Nor do I think of the cost to the environment, or of the archetypal conflict – Man versus Nature; rather, my mind is consumed with the thought of all the money that I am about to make. As those in charge drone on about the wildland-urban interface, how humans have jammed their lives into box canyons and smeared the forests with their houses and communities and ribbons of road and the risks thereof, all I hear is the flap of dollars being stacked in my bank account, with every mention of tragedy, I calculate, and give thanks for, the overtime that I am about to receive.

"And behold, the smoke of the land

ascended like the smoke of a furnace."

Genesis 20:28

The Highlands 20 see smoke. Brownish-whitish smoke hemorrhages from a mountaintop, a gaseous python writhing into the clear blue sky. Traffic moves. Barely. We are Eastbound on Highway 2 between Cashmere and Wenatchee and we are at the mercy of every gawking vehicle ahead of us. As we round the bend, we see fire. The mountain to our right is consumed with fast moving orange flames that gain life with every wind gust. We are fresh and keyed-up. An hour earlier we were at the closing ceremonies of the ten-day conference of wildland firefighters at Central Washington University, where they thanked us for our participation and wished us luck, and now here we are face-to-face with the very thing we want to see most. The fire represents many things to us – a challenge, an enemy, an adventure, an incident, a job, a destroyer, a noble cause, a paycheck.

We watch the land burn, licking our lips, waiting for dispatch to give the word, to speak over the handheld radio and assign us to the fire that is within reach, for without their permission we can do nothing. But their permission never comes. Our proximity is of no consequence. What is of consequence is that this is the very beginning of the fire season and we are not in our district, at best our district is another ninety minutes away. Despite our successful ten-days of wildfire training and our hunger to battle the flames that are within reach, the Highlands 20 are not chosen for this blaze. Another fire crew, one from the district we're driving through, gets assigned to the fire.

Such are the territorial ways of the wildland firefighting world.

The black of night engulfs us. The air is heavy and smells of burning forest. Smoke hugs the earth and crawls down the mountainside. The Highlands 20 are assigned to the Sandy's North Fire. It's our first incident of the summer and every man is eager to eat smoke, to earn blisters, to not complain, to prove himself.

We arrive long after the sun has set, and our only source of light is the bright beams jutting out from the headlamps strapped to our helmets. Our mission starts like most all others: digging fireline (carving an 18-inch wide line down to bare earth around the perimeter the fire) from an anchor point, a place we feel confident the fire won't jump across.

From the one-lane gravel road our buggies are parked on we hack our way up the darkened slope. Each man follows in the footsteps of the man before him. The murmur of curse words mingle with the sounds of metal whacking dirt, whacking rock, whacking root, and when we reach the hilltop, and tie into the black (connect our fireline to the already burnt area of the fire), we get off our feet and gulp water.

After assessing the situation it's decided that we perform a backburn, i.e., fighting fire with fire (a tactic used to eliminate potential fuel [dead and downed trees, branches, logs, etc.] from a wildfires path by burning it).

It is our first backburn of the summer and the crew's excitement is palpable. Driptorches are assembled with a certain lust. To put it bluntly, each of us has a 'fire boner,' as was explained to me, is a metaphor for the near erotic charge one feels when fighting wildfire. With driptorches lit, "burners" - our name for those who use the driptorches - start dropping fire between our fresh dug fireline and the creeping wildfire, working their way down the mountain in a zigzag pattern.

At 2 a.m. the mission is complete. The wildfire is contained. All potential fuel is destroyed. The driptorches are spent, and so are we, but with it comes a feeling of accomplishment and solidarity, a knowing that, we, as a fire crew, are up for whatever challenges lay ahead. As we spread our sleeping bags in a grassy field beside Highway 395 beneath the clear and endless sky, we fall asleep knowing that whatever the fire season brings we will accomplish it together.

This, knowing, however, doesn't last long.

There is something uneasy in the Washington air this July morning, some strange aura, some apprehension. It is our sixth or seventh fire of the summer; even this early on it's hard to keep track. We've been running and gunning from fire-to-fire-to-fire-to-fire since June, and the rising sun spills over the mountaintop, giving light, heating the land and all that walk upon it.

The Highlands 20 are at an ICP (Incident Command Post), a campground overlooking the Columbia River turned makeshift basecamp for firefighting resources, and in every direction wildland firefighters are rushing, gathering, loading, fueling, sharpening - preparing themselves, their tools, and their vehicles for the day's fight with Nature.

It's half past seven and we load up into our buggies. For a moment all seems fine, normal.

It isn't.

There is a problem.

We do a head count. We're one man short. We exit our buggies intent on finding Jonah, the missing.

It doesn't take long.

He's in the midst of a small circle; surrounding him, our three squadbosses and crewboss. Jonah's eyes: downcast, his hands, buried in his pants pockets. He kicks at the dirt as he talks. We can't hear him, but based on the other four men's body language – arms crossed over chests, rigid mouths, eyes locked on Jonah – what he's saying is not pleasing.

A few tense minutes pass before our squadboss has us load back into our buggies, minus Jonah, and we head out for today's mission. Not even three weeks into our already intense fire season and we're down one man. The Highlands 20 is now the Highlands 19.

My fire crew responds to the Valley Chapel Fire and is the first resource on scene. We are the ONLY resource on scene. There are no other resources available. It's still the beginning of the fire season and wildland firefighters are already spread cellophane thin.

Our crewboss hikes up the hostile mountainside to scout the fire as the rest of the crew buzzes with anticipation, strapping on linepacks, readying tools, readying themselves - chugging water and scarfing protein bars. It's a quarter to four in the afternoon and the sun is nowhere close to setting. The July heat is intense, we're not even moving and we're already flooded with sweat.

When our crewboss returns, he gives a quick and dirty briefing.

Our mission: indirect attack, carve a fireline into the earth from our position up to the black then perform a backburn and burn the fuel between us and the flame front.

Using the two-lane blacktop as our anchor point, we cut fireline, ripping and hacking and chinking our way inch-by-inch up the rocky steepness.

Hours pass. Backs, bent and aching. Heads, down. We've been digging fireline for so long my shoulders have gone from loose to stiff to loose again, and at this moment I'm fueled by adrenaline alone. Before I realize it's gone, the sun slides behind the mountain, leaving us in its shaded wake, and providing mild relief.

We're a hard earned mile from where we started and the smell of burning timber is so strong I can taste it on my tongue. It is here and now that we get eyes on the fire. It's maybe 30 feet away, gently backing down the mountain.

Then as quick as fingers snapping together the stale air bursts to life, wind screams down the mountain and whips through the trees. It blows thick smoke in our faces - eyes pinch shut; tears compensate for the sudden dryness.

The fire, pushed by the raging wind, charges toward us; gathering strength, growing from 12-inch to 30-inch flame lengths in the span of a pulse.

"RTO!" (Reverse Tool Order) is shouted from our squadboss. It's an order that means we have been compromised, that the fire is moving toward us with such speed, such ferocity that we must reverse ourselves down the mountain before the wildfire overtakes us.

There's no time to feel, no time to think. There's only time to act. We turn on our heels and reverse ourselves down the mountain; down the fireline we've just dug, down our escape route as the fire devours the terrain we fought so hard to protect.

It is late July and we're racing across Washington State to our next wildfire. This summer the State's been burning nonstop, which means the Highlands 20 have been battling Nature nonstop. I feel it, too - my body, my soul – every part of me is worn out. I can count on one hand how many days we've had off, and still have fingers to spare. At this point I've lost track of the number of incidents we've been on. Each wildfire bleeds into the next forming a blur of hiking and cursing and fire and pain.

It's mid-day, but you wouldn't know it. Outside my window I see darkness. The wildfires are so abundant, the smoke of which so dank, so rich with black soot and cancerous particles that it swallows the sunlight, turning day into night.

I have fifty more days on my contract and with every wildfire that we respond to I am expected to perform at my peak, to be fully aware, to give my all. But at this moment I feel that I have nothing left to give. I feel like my precious State, as if my daylight, too, has been overwhelmed by darkness.

All the bravado I began this fire season with is now gone. In its place, survival instincts, a need to ignore pain, ignore exhaustion, to carry on.

On the outskirts of Loomis is a piece of scrap wood painted with the Stars and Stripes and below it are the words:

Thank you, firefighters. God bless you!

This fire season God's blessings are in high demand, and not just by firefighters, but by the entire State, and the way things are going it doesn't seem like he's doling them out very generously.

My mind is a unique machine filled with vignettes and sensations and names and faces and locations, but what fills the cracks in my grey matter, the connective tissue that links all of these aspects into pulsing living memory are dates and times. I recall the blood-red glow of the digital clock when I lost my virginity, 7:07 p.m. The date that I said adios to America for two years to adventure through Asia: June 21, 2010. The exact time was 8:29 a.m. when I read an email awarding me a vacation to Nicaragua. The last day of my last class of my university career - December 6, 2016.

I can also summon with great clarity the date and time that I learned three wildland firefighters had perished not far from where I was standing: August 19, 2015 – 7:21 p.m.

The air we breathe is choked with gray smoke. The sun, blood red, cuts a perfect circle through the opaque sky. The air sags with ash and soot and clings to our bodies; our every inhale holds weight. Our once cherry red buggies are parked in a clearing and have taken on a pinkish hue, covered in layers of dusky grit. Around the clearing are trees, scorched black, the fire having eaten away needles and limbs, leaving behind a legion of sharpened spikes in their place.

The Highlands 20 are beat down, filth covered, and on the tail end of a sixteen-hour shift, loading our linepacks and tools into the buggies.

With our gear stowed, one of our squadbosses has us circle around him for an end of day debrief. The news he gives us is a cruel exclamation point to an already brutal shift on the fireline. He gives it to us straight: three wildland firefighters had been burnt over a few hours prior. Faces are tight. No tears are shed. No soft words are spoken for the departed. They knew the risks, just like every wildland firefighter does. There is less of a sense of loss amongst our fire crew than there is a combined feeling of sympathy and relief. Sympathy for the poor bastards that lost their lives earning slightly more than a McDonald's worker in Seattle, and relief that it wasn't any of us.

There is a large wooden sign at the entrance of the Highlands 20 Fire Camp:

Home of
Highlands 20
Better Than Water

I thought long and hard about this, if it is true, if 20 men with chainsaws and Pulaskis (tools used to dig fireline) and grit are better than water. Most fire seasons I believed that we were, but this summer I have my doubts.

It is two o'clock on a Friday afternoon in August and it's hot and dry and the air so thick with smoke that if one didn't know better you would think that the pines and firs and tamaracks are shrouded in mist. The Highlands 20 are back at our summer home, back at our Fire Camp outside of Loomis, Washington after a fourteen day rotation and are ready for our one day off before we go back into the wild lands and fight fire.

Three of us have plans to get away from the crew for our R&R day, to spend our sacred 24-hours off away from "the boys" and in the company of women, as there is a limit to the amount of "man time" one can handle without punching someone in the face.

We're in the barracks putting on civilian attire – shorts and t-shirts - and our squadboss enters. He's all business. He rallies us to circle up by the picnic tables outside. There he relays the following: our Fire Camp is being threatened by fire a few miles south and the winds are pushing it right to our front door. He knows that some of us are planning an exodus and gives us a choice. Those who want to leave, leave now. Those who stay, defend Fire Camp.

Forest, Jacob and I share a look and instantly reach the same conclusion: fuck Fire Camp. Before our squadboss can renege on his offer we're in Jacob's Chevy Blazer, gas pedal - floored, wheels spitting gravel, the Highlands 20 Fire Camp in the rearview mirror.

We woke this morning to a crimson sun bleeding through the thick skin of smoke that blanketed the land, ash drifting from the sky, coating us like dirty snowflakes. A few days prior I witnessed a fire whirl, where erratic winds whipped the fire from multiple directions, spinning it into a vertical and hellish cylinder that danced across the landscape.

This summer we've have seen so much wildfire that nothing fazes us. Five miles later that all changes.

Behind us: the Highlands 20 Fire Camp, the winding two-lane Sinlahekin Road banded on both sides by dense forest, and the one saloon town of Loomis. Ahead: flat fields of alfalfa. The mountain to the west is an inferno, screaming with the colors of fire. Being driven before the flames are a horde of animals – whitetail deer, black bear, field mice, squirrels, elk, mountain lions, big horn sheep. No longer predator. No longer prey. They flee together in a herd-size chunk across the open land as if the flaming mountain is evicting them. They bolt across the blacktop to the safety of the yet unburnt mountain to the east. It is something I can never un-see. It is a scene from the bible come to life. It is apocalypse now.

August 22, 2015 is a sun scorched and arid day in North Central Washington, the kind of day where wildfire flourishes and the air smells of burning and it is a long way from the snow and cold, a long way from winter, a long way from relief. Elsewhere in the world, the second-in-command of ISIS is killed in a drone strike in Iraq. Four passengers, including two off-duty military servicemen, foil a gunman's attack on a high-speed train from Amsterdam to Paris. The Dow Jones Industrial Average falls 500 points. An armed veteran sneaks into a New York federal building, fatally shoots a security guard, before taking his own life, and, President Obama approves federal emergency aid for Washington State wildfires.

And, in Okanogan County, in North Central Washington, the

Highlands 20 saves a small town from being burned off the map.

The day begins as a commonplace enough day on a wildfire, one of those days where your hips grind in their sockets from the countless miles you've hiked, your knees are battered and feel as if they may give out on you at any moment, your back moans from the weight of your linepack, the months of sleeping on rocky ground, and your brain is so sick of thinking of nothing but fire that it sets your teeth on edge. What you need is rest, but rest you are not to have. You have a job to do so you lace up your boots, strap on your linepack, chug water, and do the damn thing.

There's wildfire in the sagebrush heavy hills above Tonasket, Washington and the Highlands 20's mission for the day is simple: stop the fire before it gets to the town. If we fail and the wildfire wins chances are Tonasket will be nothing more than a puff of smoke and blackened skeletons where buildings once stood.

A dozer (bulldozer) line is already torn into the earth, in an attempt to keep the wildfire at bay. Our plan: backburn from the dozer line, drop fire of our own onto the ground, destroy the fuel between the fire and us.

At noon we leave our buggies and hike into the fawn-colored hills with our tools and driptorches and aches and pains. The heat of the day breathes across the arid landscape. The wind is blistering and sooty and does not bring relief. And at this point in the fire season I no longer feel like I'm the best. I feel the toll that wildland firefighting has taken on my body, feel it more than the rest of the Highlands 20 as I understand without a doubt that age is not just a number, that I am a solid decade or more older than the rest of my fire crew, and I don't bounce back like I used to. And yet I carry on, huffing, puffing, cursing, spitting, sweating, pushing myself upward, onward.

At the dozer line we do a few test strips, dropping fire on the ground to ensure the conditions are ripe for our backburn. They are not. The wind drives our small fire away from the incoming wildfire and onto the dozer line. The decision is made to wait until the air gusts in our favor. We hike back to our buggies. We eat. We sleep. We hydrate. We wait.

The sun is long gone and the moon is up, hiding behind the smoke that cloaks the earth. The blackness that is around is a comfort as with it comes the cool of night. The rest has helped. I am no longer plagued by my age and we are back on the dozer line, and this time when we drop fire the wind rushes in the direction we want.

On nearly every wildfire that we have been on this fire season we've backburned, as a result two things are apparent. One, backburning no longer thrills. We've grown complacent, bored of fighting fire with fire. This is a hazardous attitude for wildland firefighters to have, but it is the attitude that we have, a byproduct of a fire season where there are too many wildfires and too few resources, and where those resources must backburn at every opportunity to gain the upper hand.

The second byproduct becomes apparent through recall. The Highlands 20 dropped so much fire on the ground in the summer of 2015 that it's hard to distinguish one wildfire from the other as they all meld into the same series of sensations – hiking, slinging fire, feeling the heat of flame on your naked face, the choking smell of smoke, gallons of sweat racing out of your body.

But this backburn is different. The stakes are higher. We are not deep in a forest on a tract of land far from humans, we are only a few miles from a town of a thousand people, people who don't know it, but who are depending on us to succeed, to beat Nature.

For hours and hours and miles and miles we hike and burn, and burn and hike. Our fire roars up and over the dry sagebrush, burning in quick hot flashes, and since the night is smoke-choked black and starless, once our backburn dies down it leaves orange pockmarks on the otherwise darkened terrain that eventually snuff out from lack of flammable nourishment.

At 5am the black of night dissolves to the smoky-blue-gray of early morning.

Our mission is complete.

Chalk up a win for the Highlands 20.

Tonasket does not burn.

For days, for weeks, for months the Highlands 20 are assigned to one fire after another and we see mountains and valleys and plains burn, and we joke about how we're living through the end times. Washington State in the summer of 2015 is a State of catastrophe, of Armageddon, and, just as reliable as the destructive hurricane seasons in the Southeast of the United States determines how life is lived there, so the volatility and randomness of wildfires influence the quality of life in Washington State, emphasize its vulnerability, how fragile our existence is. This fire season, more than any other, shows us how close we are to the brink of breaking, how close I am to the brink of breaking.

2018

The Chainsaw

Me and the chainsaw on the Jon Tom Fire (2013).
Photo Credit: Jeff Cedarbaum.

The chainsaw is a tool for cutting smoothly through material that needs to be hewn asunder. You, a sawyer, are a man, and wielder of the chainsaw, using it do your bidding the same way a sorcerer commands spirits to do his. Separate, and you are nothing, mere pieces in the puzzle of wildland firefighting. United, you become something bigger than the sum of your parts. You form an alliance of man and tool and become destroyers: the nemesis of wildfire.

The chainsaw is never to be forced. It is to be sharpened and respected. If you brandish it properly, wood chips fly, the wood parts - and in its wake you create: two where there was previously one - the burning end of the tree branch is no longer a threat.

To accomplish this: you hold the chainsaw as you do a woman or a double barrel shotgun – tight, close to your body, and with both hands. Your fingers must never be loose, but constantly squeezing tight with the thumb wrapped around the front handle.

When you and the chainsaw are in the moment, acting as one, you will be overcome with a calmness that flows from your mind and encompasses your entire being. Do not be alarmed at the absence of fear. Fear is still present it is merely quieted. This stillness that you feel comes only through rote training, so when crisis arrives it is that same learned tranquility that allows you and the chainsaw to cut quickly and smoothly through whatever is between you and the fire.

No matter how many cuts you make, how many trees and

branches you separate from each other, you will find yourself in awe of the chainsaw: hot, sharp, loud, oil-stained. At times you will find it hard to distinguish where you end and the chainsaw begins. Never forget that you and that pot-bellied cleaver in your hands have come together for a benevolently violent purpose: the dissecting of Nature in order to save Nature.

Make no mistake; your entry into Nature is definitely a violent one, still, it is quite tame when compared to the fierceness of a wildfire. Soon after cuts are made, and the fuel (material that could burn) has been removed from the fireline you have just cleared, you will be joined by the rest of your fire crew using Pulaskis, Rhinos, and other manpowered fire tools until the fireline you have cut blooms into an eighteen-inch wide swath of upturned bare earth that outlines the perimeter of the fire.

When you and the chainsaw are one, all your five senses will be fully engaged - the gritty, acrid taste of ash as you run your tongue across your teeth; your nostrils will fill with a foul bouquet: an amalgamation of aged-salted-sweat and timber smoke; you will feel the gravity of your linepack, pulling you into the earth on which you stand, the heat of the flames on the soft flesh of your neck and ears, the humming bulk of the mechanical beast in your grip. There are also thrilling and jolting sounds: the satisfying growl that occurs when the chainsaw comes to life in your hands, the high pitched whine followed by an almost immediate thwack as the chain comes off the bar and hurls itself into your Kevlar protected thighs (thereby not ravaging your leg meat), the recitation of curse words that become so common you use them whether your spirit is fouled or elated. You will see colors as you have never seen them before. The opaque gray of the smoke, the primeval green of the timber, the infernal orange and red and yellow of the fire – as the fire backs down the mountain it eats greedily at the green, chewing up living forest, leaving behind black destruction. It must be stopped. The green that represents life must be separated from the hot flames with its sharp fangs, breathing hot and heavy down their neck. The chainsaw howls and cuts. Behind you hands move in unison, throw, chop, dig, scrape. You and your fire crew will work as one, the same as you and the chainsaw, fully engaged with the task at hand.

If you are observant, you will find the veil between active military life and that of being a wildland firefighter is vellum thin. In your first few weeks you are inundated with terms, vernacular, and chains of command, all done with the utmost sincerity. What follows are weeks and weeks of training that prepare you for the physical, mental, and emotional sacrifices that will need to be made. Finally, you find yourself at the forefront of the battle; only this battle is not against man, but Nature, out on the fireline, where every bit of knowledge gained will be put to the test. In place of camouflage fatigues or body armor, Nomex pants and shirt and a hard helmet are your uniform. You do not go into battle armed with an M4, but the chainsaw.

In wildland firefighting there are no purple hearts or medals of valor. There is only the fire and you, made of flesh and bone and blood. And in this battle with Nature, just as in battles with a human enemy, it is to the death. To the victor go the spoils, and in this case the spoils of war is life itself.

And yet there are times when the fire is not quelled by your meager attempts of attacking it with the chainsaw. It burns even more furiously, and as if in defiance of being snuffed out of existence, the fire moves swiftly from tree crown to tree crown, igniting tree after tree in an endless arc of orange anarchy. For the first time you understand that you and the chainsaw, despite coming together as one, are no match for the wall of flames consuming the forest. Your tool seems primitive when faced with the reality of what needs to take place. As you sit and feed the chainsaw fuel and oil, and prepare it for battle by sharpening its chain, you hear the unmistakable low rumble of a DC-10 Tanker coming over the horizon before its belly splits open and paints the infuriated forest with a cloud of maroon, white, or turquoise retardant, ably quelling the flames that you and the chainsaw could not. As the fire-killing powder settles onto the flames putting a damper on their carnage, the vista takes on an almost familiar visage. Half-burnt trees stand side-by-side with those that are untouched by flame, like a before and after picture caught in real time.

You pull off your leather gloves, take off your helmet, and run a dirty hand over your sweat-drenched brow – relief. You go into the forest twice as filthy as the day before and twice as determined to accomplish your mission. You symbolize both the pleasant and unpleasant this world has to offer, which must coexist, occasionally slipping into chaos.

You and the chainsaw are adventurers in wild lands, pushing upward and onward into an arid and hellish landscape, making order out of turmoil. It is a glorious time for the senses, each of them intensified by the rush of adrenaline. With every step forward danger increases. Mind and body must focus on the chainsaw's cuts that lay before you; you must accomplish the mission, suppress the wildfire. Together you are the tools that save the Division.

Situational awareness will become your second nature. Look up. Look down. Look around. A catface snag. Smoke barrels out from the charred hole in its side, an invisible dragon in a blackened cave. Be careful as the chainsaw touches this burnt and still burning tree. The wrong cut and it might turn on you, drop on you, crushing you with the sudden impact of wood on flesh. You must calculate where the most efficient cut should go, and make sure to leave enough holding wood for it to fall where you intend. The eyes look up and tally the limbs, their approximate weight, and how their positioning will affect your felling operation and where you want it to land. The eyes then scan the surrounding area for escape routes, taking quick mental notes of several in case the tree does not cooperate and instead intends to fall back on you; at the same time checking your cutting area to make sure it is free of both foliage and human obstacles. Then, and only then, do you call out to where you intend to fell the catface snag, a warning that needs to be loud enough for all in the area to remove themselves from potential danger.

With a pull of the starter cord the chainsaw is alive in your hands. You place the guide bar on the bark and make your first cut, followed by an adjoining cut at a 45-degree angle. This is your pie cut. The wedge of the pie cut falls to the ground as you swiftly reposition yourself and the chainsaw for your back cut, the whole time keeping your neck craned toward the sky, always aware of your tree and where it might fall. The chainsaw cuts through the scorched remains of the tree with ease, stopping as you see the top of the dead tree begin to tip in the direction you had intended. Without looking back, you remove the chainsaw and exit the cutting area via one of the escape routes you have already surveyed. The squeal of the wood as it falls is capped off with the thundering wallop of it crashing to the earth. Before you, what was once a threat is safety incarnate.

What follows are a few quick seconds of silence. You look at what you have done; the once mighty and menacing tree now lies passively on its side, and you bask in the adrenaline rush of having overcome Nature. Your Swamper, the person assigned to assist you, claps you on the shoulder, “Good cutting, Brother.”

Before you can reply a call comes across your swamper’s handheld radio. It is your squadboss. You are to hike back to the crew. Direct attack on the fire is to commence posthaste.

“Copy. On our way,” is what your Swamper replies. No time to sheathe the chainsaw, you hoist it onto your shoulder as your swamper gathers the dual two-stroke gas and oil canister, threads it through the handle of his swamper tool and slings it over his shoulder.

Within thirty seconds of receiving the call the two of you are trudging up the mountain. As you climb to the peak, your Swamper says, “Have I ever told you about the time that I dated a chick who loved to be choked?” You tell him no, even though you have heard that story so many times this fire season, you sometimes get it confused as one of your own memories. It is not your favorite story, or even one that you feel comfortable hearing, but it takes your mind off the task at hand, and the task to come, off of what moments from now will be expected of you and the chainsaw.

At the mountain’s peak you meet your squadboss, soot covered and smoking a cigarette. You wonder how anyone can practically run up steep inclines with 45 lbs. on their back and a 5 lb. tool in their hand and still the have lung capacity to smoke a cigarette. He flicks the ash from his cigarette and has your squad circle around him. His voice is level, professional. “We got a call from the Div. Sup. (Pronounced: Div-Soop) He wants us over on Division Charlie which is here,” he points at a location on a topographical map resting on a stump. He sucks down a final drag before flicking his cigarette. “The fire is backing down through some heavy timber and a hell of a lot of dead and down. The reported flame lengths are ten inches. Our mission is to attack it from the head and tie into that logging road,” again he points at the map. “If need be, we have permission to burn off from the road. Hazards are going to be the usual: rolling rocks and debris, snags, and there’ve been reports of bees in that area. So you with the EpiPens, keep em’ handy. That’s all I got. Any questions? Concerns?”

There are none. You all know the score. You know what is expected of you and the chainsaw. Within minutes you are in STO (Standard Tool Order – chainsaws followed by Pulaskis then Rhinos) hiking close behind your squadboss. As you cross your Division en route to your new position you witness the ashen carnage left by the fire. For as far as you can see the forest floor is gray. With every step ash rises to meld with your clothes, your flesh; it gets into the fissures of your teeth and you feel its grit every time that you drink from the nipple of your CamelBak. All the trees you see no longer resemble the lush green royals that they once were; instead they look like gigantic blackened spears thrust into the mountainside. The only word that comes to mind is: nuked.

After crossing the dead zone you once again reach living forest. From here you see the plume of smoke, where you are needed, where your mission waits. The entire hike to the head of the fire your mind is not on you or the chainsaw, but on the girl you left at home and what she is doing at this exact moment. Is she working a shift at Walmart? Is she at the lake with her friends? Is she…but before you can finish the thought you are where you need to be, where you and the chainsaw were destined to be.

You do not hesitate. You know exactly what to do, for you have trained for hours and hours for this exact moment. You and the chainsaw move as one, no longer man and tool, but a functioning unit intent on separating the burnt from the unburnt. The chainsaw's sharpened chain is unimpeded by brush or branches. Stress simmers out of you in the form of sweat. Through the PVC of your earplugs you hear the constant snarl emanating from the oily metallic beast in your hands. The wood splits with its own kind of snarl. It howls in defiance. Tree branches – from ground level to shoulder height – are sawed off; if the trees are too small they are sliced off at the base, the dead and down are lopped into manageable pieces; and out of the oily shadows of your mind this thought occurs: it is not I that is using the chainsaw, but the chainsaw that is using me.

The wind blows and the fire seeks revenge, eating more forest, choking you with more smoke. Still, you persevere.

You and the chainsaw have followed the head of the fire up and down and all around the mountain and finally you see your end point, your place of respite: the old logging road.

After the battle with Nature, you and the chainsaw are resting. The fiery squall is restrained. The colossal roaring fire is put to sleep by an eighteen-inch earthen line dug by the men who followed the path you cut for them. Man and tool have won: mission accomplished. Beside you, the chainsaw is lifeless, out of fuel; its chain is dull, bar oil and blackened sawdust cling to its haunches. But you cannot let it stay dead. You must resurrect the chainsaw, and so you do, with drink of oil and guzzle of fuel, a sharpening of the chain, and a wipe off of the muck: for you understand that the chainsaw is more than a tool used for cutting smoothly through material that needs to be hewn asunder, it is what gives you purpose.

2018

The ABCs of Fire Season

A backburn during a night ops (nighttime operation) on the Sandy's North Fire (2015).

Left to right: Carlton and Patty

<u>Alicia</u>

The prettiest gal in Okanogan County; in fact she was the only pretty gal in all of North Central Washington in the summer of 2013. The Cali Boys and I met her at the Breadline Café on one of our nights off in the illustrious town of Omak. With eyes of creamy jade and flax-brown hair, she was sassy and bubbly – sassy in character and bubbly in body type. All summer long she put up with our blunt childish attempts at flirtation and made us all believe in love at first sight.

Beechnut breakfast

When a wildland firefighter skips breakfast and instead fills their mouth with the sweet molasses flavor of loose leaf chewing tobacco.

CamelBak bukkake

July 9th, 2013 finds the Highlands 20 on the HWY 155 Fire on the Colville Indian Reservation. We, the saw team, finish a direct attack, cutting sagebrush away from the fire's edge, and are fueling and oiling and sharpening our chainsaws, as the rest of the Highlands 20 finishes digging fireline. The sun is hot and drops heavy from the sharp blue sky, heating the earth, and us, past the point of comfort. There is no wind to speak of. The only bit of oasis in this desert heat is the cool of sweat evaporating from our flesh.

Billy, squad two's sawyer (chainsaw operator), lifts his helmet, runs a filthy forearm across his sooty brow, and says, "I don't know about you, but I sure could go for a CamelBak (hydration pack) bukkake right about now."

His words immediately cut a clear and soggy image. I envision nineteen of the Highlands 20, CamelBak hoses in hand, circled around a kneeling Billy, squirting his dirt-riddled face with spurts of water.

And in that moment, with my throat as dry as sawdust, and tinkles of sweat oozing out of my every pore, I, too, could go for a CamelBak bukkake.

Don't be a pussy

Frenchie, a swamper (assistant to a sawyer), an ex-Navy man, and champion mayonnaise eater, always used the phrase, "Don't be a pussy," anytime a crewmember of the Highlands 20 grumbled about hiking up ungodly steep mountains, or not getting enough sleep, or having to eat MRE's (dehydrated and tasteless foodstuffs of soldiers), or not getting a shower, or a rank fart, or working too much, or working too little, or sore feet, or a sore back, or sore knees, or a broken heart, or missing friends and family, or being stopped up from MRE's, or its opposite: "Judy booty," also known as, diarrhea – it was pretty much his given answer for any bellyaching from the crew. It was meant to insult, in a brotherly way; meant to put your manhood in check so as to rise above the discomfort at hand and carry on.

It became a crew mantra, and one that I use to this day; whether I'm stopped up or not.

Eagle Fire

It's August 19, 2013, and the Highlands 20 arrives at the Eagle Fire at five in the afternoon. The air is ninety-four degrees, dry, and carries the sweet pine scent of a warm forest. The yellow sun through the tall pines cast flecks of light and shadow all around. Rotors (helicopters) chud-chud-chud overhead, streaking through the sky; their bright orange buckets suspended by cables and heavy with water. Handheld radios squawk with voices giving details of the fire – incident size, expected winds, weather conditions. From the peak of the mountain fat ribbons of opaque smoke rise vertically into the atmosphere.

We don our linepacks, grab our tools, and circle up around the hood of the buggies where our crewboss briefs us on our mission: hike up the mountain to the fireline and perform a direct attack (construct a fireline on a fire's edge to suppress its fuel [logs, branches, bushes, etc.] consumption). Amongst the Highlands 20 there is less of a sense of excitement, since we've done this numerous times over the course of the fire season, and more of a feeling of having to find our second wind, as we have already worked eleven hours on the Stemilt Fire before being reassigned here.

The renewed energy we're looking for hits us hard and fast like a syringe of adrenaline punched into our hearts as we hike at a pulse-pounding, knee-cracking speed to the top of the mountain. The mountain I speak of is a certain type of steep that can only be described as sharp. The soil of which is also sandy; every step upwards feels as if we slide back two. Not even ten minutes into our trek the wind does an about-face, forcing the smoke down slope, into our faces, into our lungs. Sweat rains from us. Curses gush from our mouths - curses to drive each other further, upwards and onwards, curses at the mountain itself, and curses just for the sake of cursing.

After two miles of near-perpendicular hiking we reach the source of the smoke: the flame front. The flame lengths are around 12 inches and back down the mountainside through ankle high green grass and a sprawl of dead and down trees. The other sawyer and I remove our chainsaw's condoms (bar covers), pull start them to growling, howling life and begin cutting an eight-foot swath of potential fuel away from the fire's edge, working our way up the mountain as we go. Behind us the rest of the Highlands 20 start forging fireline, digging down to mineral soil, separating the remaining ground fuel from the fire itself. The smoke, once thick, is now practically chunky in texture. Tears surge from my stinging eyes. Strings of snot burst from my nostrils. My lungs burn from the toxins released by the smoke. Every few yards I drop to my knees to suck in as much cool air as I can at ground level before rising to my feet and carrying on with the mission.

Day becomes night as we crest the mountaintop and tie (connect our fireline) into the black (the already burnt area of the fire). We sit. We rest. We eat. All around are the charred remains of a once thriving forest. Giant pines scorched thin and black, creak and sway in the wind. Tangles of burning embers illuminate naked and cadaverous fir trees. We wait for orders to head back down to our buggies. The order never comes. Instead our mission gets extended. We are to stay put and monitor the fire to ensure that burning debris does not roll downhill and cause a spot fire in the green (the unburnt area) below our position.

Our squadbosses separate us into groups of three and instruct us to keep each other awake throughout the night. The night grows dark and the stars shimmer against its silky blackness. The wind increases in speed. The temperature drops. Our once sweaty, pliable Nomex (fire resistant shirts and pants) are rawhide stiff. My group of three huddles together for warmth; too cold to sleep, too tired to stay awake, a trancelike state overtakes me and sensations rattle through my mind until dawn: the random groans and eventual thunderclap crashes of burnt trees falling around us, the pungent scent of combined dried sweat and timber smoke, the taste of soot as I run my tongue over my teeth, the feel of the forest floor we rest on still warm from the intense blaze.

Fear

In terms of fire growth and the development of dangerous situations, wildfire can go from zero to a hundred in the blink of an eye. As my squadboss used to say, "Shit gets real, real quick," and when it does you have to keep your cool, think fast, and act faster. You're not faced with terrifying circumstances constantly, but they do happen, and when "shit gets real;" you feel less a sense of fear and more of a kick in the ass from reality. From hours of rote training your brain switches to survival autopilot, you take in as much of the situation as you can, assess it, and calculate ways to keep yourself and your crew alive.

Fear, when felt, must be kept at bay. No matter how dire the situation, a wildland firefighter must always look for the positive, for a way out – even when there is none – as fear is a form of weakness and weakness leads to death, and death is never an option.

Gonzalez, Jimmy

Jimmy Gonzalez, one third of the Cali Boys, was (is) a rascal of a young man with impish brown eyes, and ever-present smile, acid wit, a graduate from Rio Hondo Fire Academy, and whose rookie fire season also happened to be my rookie fire season.

Gonzalez was lead Pulaski (a pick-lick tool used to dig fireline) and hiked behind me in STO (Standard Tool Order – Chainsaws followed by Pulaskis, followed by Rhinos [a hoe-like tool used to dig fireline]), and when we'd be tromping miles through burning forests, up severe mountainsides, and he would hear me breathe heavy curses, he'd encourage me to keep going, saying, "Come on, Chuck, it builds character."

He used to twitch anytime there were loud and unexpected noises, remnants of his time in the Marine Corps, as was his tendency to speak of "pink mist" (the pinkish misty residue, which is the blood of a target hit by a tank shell) when he had had one too many cans of malt liquor.

In complete deadpan tone, he once described fire as being, "hotter than two squirrels fucking in a wool sock."

And I'll be damned if those words don't cross my mind now every time I'm in close proximity to flames.

Hiking

On the Highlands 20 hiking and wildland firefighting are synonymous. You can't have one without the other. That is the very reason that initial attack crews (and hotshots and smokejumpers) exist, to be able to hike into the wild lands - the mountains, the forests, the canyons – all the places that cannot be reached by vehicle in order to fight wildfire.

It is foolish to think that all it takes is strength and stamina to hike up miles of near perpendicular mountainsides with a 45lb linepack on your back, and a tool in hand that weighs between 5lb to 15lbs. Just as important is strength of spirit. I admit: I am a shit hiker. I cannot hike fast. But what I lack in speed I make up for with dogged determination.

There are two hiking hacks I learned early on in my rookie fire season that helped me push through the pain, the weight, the heat. First, keep your head down and your eyes locked on the boot heels of the man in front of you. This isn't difficult because when hiking up near-sheer mountains your back and neck are bent at such an angle that it is easier to see the heels of your crewmates boots than it is to look up. Also, if you do focus on the mountain and how much farther you have to hump to the top of it, for lack of a better term, you're fucked. My second strategy is one I perfected when working on an Alaskan fishing vessel, and what I liken to astral projection. Physically, I would be there, in the moment, putting one foot in front of the other, hiking up steep terrain. Mentally, I was light-years away - on a foreign beach, getting laid, smoking weed, reliving past memories, fleshing out future fantasies. I visualized myself anywhere but hiking up whatever mountain my body was slogging up.

Incident Within an Incident

An "Incident Within an Incident" is a medical emergency or any accident that occurs during an incident (tsunami, earthquake, wildfire, etc.).

The morning of July 19, 2014, is a mixed bag of emotions for the Highlands 20. We start the day, like all days in fire season, with a morning briefing. Our crewboss tells us of the Carlton Complex and how it nearly burnt Pateros, Washington off the map, annihilating 100 homes in a manner of hours.

The news, as terrible as it is, doesn't crush our spirits as one might think, rather it becomes the catalyst that shakes loose any complacency we feel, on this, our fourteenth day on fire (our last day to fight wildfire before we're to take a mandatory, and much needed, R&R day), it sharpens our vigor and takes away any doubt that what we do matters.

We're less than eighty miles away from Pateros, on the Chiwaukum Creek Complex, a heavily forested mountain-scape area teeming with bears and white tail deer, but now an inferno sending up so much smoke it strangles the blue from the sky. Today's assignment is twofold: structure protection and direct attack. The first half of our mission requires us to remove any possible fuels (trees, brush, branches, etc.) that are close to designated homes. After securing the structures, we're to maneuver to the edge of the flame front and dig fireline along in its edge, in the hopes of killing the flames before they devour any property.

I am a sawyer (chainsaw operator) and Frenchie is my swamper (assistant to the sawyer who removes any fuel cut by the sawyer). Frenchie is in his late twenties, has hollow cheeks, a sinewy build, and a voice like a car crash. His work ethic is to go full throttle at all times, maniac style, which pushes me to do the same. We work like that for five hours, cutting tree, after limb, after bush. I cut relentlessly stopping only to refuel, re-oil, and re-sharpen my chainsaw, taking sips from my CambelBak when I do.

Then it happens.

After one such refill session I jump to my feet and see indiscernible flashes of light where fire should be. My legs weaken and I drop the chainsaw. I fall to my knees. I claw the earth to keep it from spinning out from under me, to keep the vomit inside from hurling out of me. I am dehydrated, smoke-choked, lush with sweat. I'm suffering from heat exhaustion and have to relinquish my chainsaw to Frenchie, leave the fireline, and be attended to by an EMT.

I am an incident within an incident.

Jon Holmes

I know what you're thinking, and the answer is, no, not him. The Jon Holmes I'm writing about is not the 70's era mustachioed pornstar, but my friend, and the man who got me into wildland firefighting.

In March of 2013 spring had not yet sprung in Northeast Washington, patches of dirty snow blanketed the landscape, and warmth was still a fantasy, but already I was jonesing to make money. I was 34 and it was my first year of college. I was living with my parents, eating out of their fridge, not two nickels to rub together - the embodiment of the clichéd broke college student. The way I saw it I had two legal options to make the kind of money I had in mind: the oil fields of North Dakota and wildland firefighting.

When my oilrig contacts dried up, I phoned Jon Holmes, a friend from high school and a wildland firefighter with over a decade of wildfire experience. He told me he knew a few fire crews that would be hiring. The next day my cellphone rang. It was the Highlands 20.

King, Matt

Matt King, crewboss for my three fire seasons on the Highlands 20. Soft spoken. Sly grin. The man was as tough as elephant hide. Lanky in build, with crooked teeth, piercing grey-blue eyes and sandy hair, he hiked with speed and silence like a ghost in a gale force wind. His twenty-four years in wildland firefighting gave him the grit, the know-how, the integrity, and the sense of humor to command respect. Matt had an air of intensity about him, and when he spoke, you listened. He was the type of man who still lived by a code of honor and looked you in the eyes when he shook your hand. He knew that fighting wildfire was not only an adventure, but just as importantly, a way to make money, and so he called in whatever favors he could to keep the Highlands 20 jumping from fire-to-fire-to-fire all summer long.

I trusted him with my life on numerous occasions and he never failed me, never afraid to push us to our limits nor turn down an assignment if he felt it put his crew, his boys, at risk.

Little Spokane Fire

July 07, 2015: it's early afternoon when the Highlands 20 reaches the incident and the sky is angry; dense smoke ascends from the mountain before us a dark and undulating tower. We watch as the wind shifts sharply and sheers the sooty tower in two, forcing the sagging smoke down upon us. I breathe deep and feel a weight on my chest.

We are the first to arrive on scene, which is good because this is what we do, this is what we train for, we're not just here to look like the heroes we imagine ourselves to be in our crusty Nomex (fire resistant pants and shirts) and scratched helmets, or to use wildland firefighting as a ploy to get laid, or to get special treatment from the communities we protect. No, we are an initial attack fire suppression resource and we're ready to do our job. Each man cinches up his linepack, grabs his tool, and stands in STO (Standard Tool Order – Chainsaws followed by Pulaskis followed by Rhinos). Our crewboss' briefing is short as most everything about the incident is unknown – size, fire behavior, expected winds.

Then the order is given and we're moving, all 20 of us are hiking into the unexplored fire. There is no single word to describe how I feel. I am not afraid. I am not in awe. There is nothing like the feeling of hiking into a fire that you know little to nothing about. It's a rush of chaos-adrenaline-smoke-charged-testosterone-pleasure known to the brave and stupid alike. As we're hiking I glance back at the other faces and see determined eyes, see fierce mouths knitted together neither smiling nor frowning. I know we all share one thing: we are all hell-bent on overtaking this fire and not letting it overtake us.

We perform an indirect attack, starting from the trail we hiked in on, and dig fireline up the vertical slope, scoring the earth with our tools – chopping through root and bush and rock and tree. And as the last tool scrapes down to mineral soil and connects to the black (the burnt area of the fire), driptorches are assembled, lit, and we drop fire of our own, attacking the flame front in my favorite way: a backburn (a tactic that involves burning the fuel - grass, weeds, branches, trees, etc. - between our fireline and the flame front, destroying any fuel that could possibly feed the wildfire).

The wind rushes behind our flames thrusting them popping, hissing, and crackling over the dried cheatgrass and boneyard of scattered dead and down trees between the wildfire and us. Then it happens, the flames we dropped collide head on with the wall of fire backing down the mountain, and for a beautiful, destructive moment they meld into one and charge skyward like an angry orange fist.

<u>Marifian, Andy</u>

Andy was (is) another third of the Cali Boys. He's lean, had rust colored hair, did pull ups for fun and talked like he was from the mean streets of Compton, but looked like he should be cast in an oatmeal commercial. He, too, was a graduate from Rio Hondo Fire Academy and his rookie fire season was my rookie fire season. He hated when we called him Andy and insisted on Andrew, but no one cared, so Andy it was. When doing difficult physical tasks – hiking, digging fireline, PT (Physical Training) – he'd yell out, "Easy," a way to motivate himself, and to prove his mettle to the rest of the crew.

The things that stick in your mind about another human are a mystery to me. For instance, after all the conversations we shared, I remember with the clarity of a flawless diamond what Andy said to me, in regards to the female population of North Central Washington, "I don't want no gals. I want some bitches"

Classic Marifian.

Nuked

A term used by wildland firefighters to describe the ravages of wildfire upon the land. Where before there had been fertile fields and thick forests of green, there are now charred and dead trees that resemble black knives stabbed into scorched and smoking soil.

Overtime

The one thing that all wildland firefighters have in common is a love of money. I don't mean that in a slimy-greed-is-good kind of way, if so, they damn sure chose the wrong line of work. What I mean is that though they may love their profession, it is still a job and one done for

American greenbacks – to feed families, to keep a roof over their heads, to repay student loans, to buy pretty gals drinks, and to one day pay alimony to those same pretty gals.

I haven't met a wildland firefighter yet who didn't want to make big bucks by the end of a fire season, who didn't calculate to the minute how much overtime was due them, and who didn't already have that money spent before it ever hit their checking accounts.

And to clock those big paychecks a wildland firefighter needs one thing: overtime, O.T., O.Ts (pronounced Oats). You might work longer hours, but your pay stub reflects such. Any hours worked over 40 in one week is overtime.

There's another fact about why wildland firefighters crave overtime: respect. The amount of overtime one gets reflects both money made and how much suffering one can endure. And if a wildland firefighter can push through to the end of long a fire season filled with hundreds of hours of O.T., which translates into hundreds of hours on your feet – humping up mountains, digging fireline, dropping fire on the ground – you gain admiration, not from the public at large who have no knowledge of the dangers and difficulties you've lived through, but from your peers.

Post lookouts when there is possible danger (Standard Firefighting Order #5)

A Lookout is one of the most important jobs on a wildland firefighting crew. As the name implies, you are a lookout, you keep eyes on your crew, on the fire, on incoming weather, other possible hazards, and then relay information if need be. The task is simple, and oftentimes boring, but doing it, and doing it well, can be the difference between lives lived and lives lost.

It's August 22, 2013 and I am a lookout on the Eagle Fire a few miles east of Leavenworth, Washington, and today I save my friend's life.

We had spent the morning hiking in and digging indirect fire line from the black (the already burnt area of the fire) to the logging road below.

Right now, I'm posted on a mountainside that overlooks the Highlands 20. I see Squad Two performing a backburn, lighting off the mountain in strips of orange flame. Below them, on the logging road, is

Squad One, my squad; they are watching the green (the unburnt area below their position) to ensure that no spot fires flare up downslope.

To the East and West of our position other fire crews perform their own missions, and as such a symphony of manual labor fills the air. The howl of chainsaws, the chud-chud-chud-chudding of rotors (helicopters) dropping buckets of water across the fire, the tink-tink-tink sound of tools digging fireline, the constant handheld radio chatter, their indiscernible conversations.

It is a hot and windy day, the fire Squad Two is dropping on the ground twists and dances across the face of the mountain as bald eagles zigzag their way back and forth against a suffocating sky. Up and down the mountain, as far as I can see, the forest is smothered in smoke. The wind howls. Embers lift off and take flight on a sudden gust. A hundred feet to the west of the fireline we stitched down the mountain, a chest high stump as big around as a barrel flashes orange and yellow, ripe with flame.

“Spot fire!” I shout into my handheld radio and give its position.

Two men, one with a chainsaw, the other with a Rhino, rush up the incline. The Rhino scoops and flings dirt onto the flames, then digs fire line around the smoldering remains. The chainsaw brings his tool to life and cuts the huge stump to an ankle height stub.

I see the stump tip over and expect it to lie still. It doesn't. The cylindrical stump rolls down the slope. The two men yell. They give chase. But their shouts are drowned out by the background noise of the other fire activity in the area, and their legs are not quick enough. The massive stump gathers speed, somersaulting end over end down the face of the mountain only making contact with the earth every few feet.

I expect it to hit the logging road and either stop or blast past it altogether to the valley below. It does neither. The fast-moving stump pitches onto the logging road, changes course as if moved by an invisible hand, doesn't lose an ounce of momentum, and barrels directly at Gonzalez who is looking out at the green, oblivious of the wooden missile locked onto him.

There's no time to radio him.

I place my hands on either side of my mouth and shout his name with all of my might, hoping it is loud enough to cut through the chainsaws, the chudding rotors, the chink of fire line construction, the squawk of the radio.

It is.

Gonzalez snaps his head uphill, sees the stump, moments away from caving in his chest, drops his tool, and shifts from left to right like a boxer in a fight, gauging his best escape route.

I grit my teeth and wince, readying myself to see my friend get smashed and killed.

Gonzalez dives over the embankment as the stump bullets past where his feet had just been planted, missing him by less than a foot.

Quitters

The Highlands 20 takes a toll on the body, mind, and soul. You spend hundreds of hours on your feet; a 45lb linepack strapped across your back. You hike up fierce mountains through less than desirable terrain. Your legs move fast and faster still. When you get to the top, the forest is engulfed in flames.

You are sweat.

You are dirt.

You are fire.

You are blood.

You are smoke.

You cut and dig fireline until the blisters on your hands and feet burst and re-form and burst again, leaving knots of unfeeling flesh in their place. Your job is to battle Nature, to stop wildfire - lives depend on it.

You sleep minimally. You work maximally. You eat food that tears your guts up, damn dietary restrictions, damn picky eaters, damn acid reflux, damn the blood in your stool, damn it all. For days into weeks, weeks into months you live like this and it wears you down, grinding you into the same blackened earth you tread upon.

And that is just the physical toll.

The mental and emotional tax is just as high, and for some, higher.

Wildland firefighting, its long days, its longer months, is an upside down way of life. It removes your focus from things that matter in 'real' life - family and friends and sports and hobbies and nightly news - and instead, it trains all of your waking thoughts and energy on the only picture that matters in that moment: the fire you are on.

With this in mind I find it astonishing that in my time as a wildland firefighter I saw only one man quit. What surprises me is that I didn't see more.

Rich Lizano

Out of the trio of Cali Boys, Rich was the oldest at 24. Graduate of Rio Hondo Fire Academy, his rookie fire season was my rookie fire season, and we were both on Squad One. He had an angular face, brown eyes, a big open smile, and square shoulders.

Over the course of the summer of 2013 we bared our souls, as one does on the Highlands 20, and in him I found a shadow of myself, in that we shared a world-weary optimism and both tended to fall in love with impossible women. His catchphrase, "Shit is weak!" was something he yelled anytime a crewmember cast shade on the hardships of wildland firefighting.

As our buggy raced across Washington State en route to the

next fire, Rich and I would be in back listening to “Stubborn Love,” by the Lumineers, a song about loving and losing an impossible woman and yet not giving up on love. Together we sang every word. We felt every word. We meant every word.

Sloan Maverick

Real name: Taylor Eggard. Square jawed, sandy spiked hair, not too long in the legs and a stocky build, he was (is) a Top Gun fanatic with the fashion sense of a frat boy, and hailed from Battleground, Washington.

He was also known as, The Fat Kid, not because he was actually fat, but because he ate like a fat kid, putting away diabetes-causing amounts of candy at every chance possible.

He was also known as, The Angry Little Man. A name given to him because of the ever-present steely look on his face, as if the burden of life was almost too much to bear, even when he joked there was a sternness about him. To his credit, he took wildland firefighting extremely seriously and used his hard-nosed outlook to fuel whatever task he was doing to the best of his ability.

Taylor wasn't always a rigid character. When he drank he transformed into his life of the party alter ego: Sloan Maverick. And by drink, I don't mean sipping on a beer, but shot-after-shot-after-shot of Irish whisky in the course of about 45 seconds. A drinking strategy I assume he picked up during his wild years at Washington State University.

Unlike Taylor, Sloan was prone to smiling as wide as a Cadillac and fits of laughter followed by bursts of humorous violence. I say humorous because his fists were never aimed at humans or animals, but rather inanimate objects – doors, windows, walls, cars, etc. As to what triggered those comically violent frenzies I can't say. We were too entertained by them to care why.

I had the pleasure of fighting wildfire with him for all three of my fire seasons on the Highlands 20.

Tragedy Fire

Tragedy fires are wildfires in which lives are lost. In my four fire seasons as a wildland firefighter, four tragedy fires occurred – the Yarnell Hill Fire, the Twisp River Fire, the Hot Pot Fire, and the Strawberry Fire.

Though the loss of life is never easy, in wildland firefighting, unless you are closely tied to the deceased their deaths are never felt by the whole. Emotion is removed and the deaths are looked upon as something to be reviewed as to not repeat the actions of the deceased.

I have five older sisters. Four of them got married. Three of them got married within a few months of meeting their husbands. Three out of three who were wed to men they barely knew had miserable marriages that ended in divorce. They were what I considered, part of the 'don't let this happen to you' crowd, public service announcements for how not to live my life.

In the same way that my sisters showed me how not to live, deaths in wildland firefighting showed me how not to die.

The deaths of wildland firefighters, as I had been taught, are meant to be stepping stones, one to grow on, a lesson learned. Each death is investigated, dissected, reported on, and then regurgitated back to the living in fire safety classes and in morning briefings. The knowledge of these deaths give you a healthy respect for the profession and the dangers involved, in the hope that you will not the same mistakes as the dead, and live to see another day.

Upper Decker

When a wildland firefighter's lower lip is so raw from too many loads of chewing tobacco that they must insert chew into their upper lip.

Valley Chapel Fire

It's the end of our sixteen-hour shift on the 4th of July 2015, and the Highlands 20 are hiking off the mountain and back to our buggies – sore muscles, bee stung, coated in sweat and ash and dirt – ready to eat a meal and fall asleep wherever we lay our weary heads. We're silent as we hike, no jokes, no ball breaking, not even any curse words, a true sign of our exhaustion. All to be heard is the chorus of our boots tromping through the forest.

About a quarter mile from our buggies the silence is broken. Whoops and hollers cut through the air. 20 pairs of eyes look across the valley to the opposite hillside, to the source of the excitement. It's a fantasy come true. Standing on the deck of a house are four bikini-clad females, waving and yelling for us to come have a beer.

As if their welcoming cheers and show of flesh isn't enough of a temptation, the soft melodic tones of *Berlin*'s, "Take My Breath Away," made famous on the Top Gun soundtrack, start drifting out of their massive outdoor speakers.

Taylor is hiking behind me, and I turn my head to ask him what he thinks about this, but I don't have to. The answer is splashed across his face like a newspaper headline. He's breathing heavily. His eyes are wide and full of longing. His jaw trembles as he mouths the lyrics, and I can only imagine that it is taking every atom of his willpower not to toss the chainsaw off of his shoulder, tear off his clothes, and sprint uphill to heed the Sirens' call.

And I think to myself, "If Taylor bolts up that house, I'm going to be two steps behind him."

You might be asking yourself why we didn't drop our tools, strip out of our crusty Nomex and hotfoot it to the ladies in waiting. The answer is simple. We couldn't. The Highlands 20 was assigned to a fire, which meant that even when we were off the clock we had to stay with our crew, to eat, to sleep, to prepare for the next day. Such is the life of a wildland firefighter.

Wizard Staff

It is a game that requires three things: canned beer, duct tape, and a thirst for large amounts of cheap brew. Actually it's not so much a game in the classical sense where there are winners and losers, but more of a drinking challenge. For starters: there are no rules of engagement. You simply drink a can of beer, and when finished, you duct tape a new beer to the top of the spent can. The goal: to build a "wizard staff" of beer cans, and have the tallest by the time everyone passes out.

Wizard Staff night was an annual event when I was on the Highlands 20 and always occurred in September when the wildfires had died down. It was always held at a nearby campground, as alcohol was not allowed at our Fire Camp.

The tallest Wizard Staff I witnessed was built from seventeen cans of Busch Light.

X's

Fire seasons ravage more than just forests and grasslands; they are destroyers of love - from casual flings to marriages with decades of mileage. Though productive for the wallet, the long hours, days, and months of having a partner all-consumed by wildfire proves devastating for those at home who love them. Every wildland firefighter I know has earned at least one failed relationship due to the job.

Yellows

Yellow is both the color and the name for the fire retardant shirts that wildland firefighters wear, and no two Yellows are the same, each tell their own story.

Bright and untarnished Yellows indicates either a rookie who hasn't earned salt-crusted-sweat-oil-dirt-soot-stains on the fireline, or a Safety Officer, whose job is to hike around to the various divisions on wildfires and monitor crews for safe work habits.

Faded and soiled Yellows imply hard work, imply veteran status, imply respect, imply someone who's been baptized in fire and smoke.

Yellows issued at the start of a fire season are typically clean and pliable. A marker for a good fire season is how plastic-hard and filthy from sweat, soot, and dirt one can make it by summer's end.

Zipp, Carlton

He was my squadboss during the 2015 fire season. Shaggy blonde hair, a shy cast to his eyes, the guy was rugged and had the frame of a lumberjack. Carlton had the ability to smoke cigarettes and then scale up mountainsides in leaps and bounds, leaving us nonsmokers in his wake.

His favorite movie was Jeremiah Johnson, and he did his best to emulate his frontier hero by not showering for weeks at a time when fighting fire, and also to save time at the end of the day so he could get as much sleep as possible. I wish I could tell you that it made him stink more than the rest of us, but truth be told: we all reeked of smoke, sweat, and musty flatulence, and his was no worse than the rest.

Carlton talked tough, and had an ever-present wad of chewing tobacco stuffed in his lower lip. He once told Cody, who had misplaced a piece of Squad Two's pump kit, "You'd lose your balls if they weren't in a sack." And followed that up with a PT hike for his entire squad, a maneuver he was notorious for – punishing the whole for the transgressions of the few.

Carlton ran his squad as if he had something to prove to himself, to the world at large, always taking on the toughest assignments when on a wildfire, often pushing his men to the brink of mutiny. At least we, his squad, talked about refusing to obey his orders, but when it came down it we never did. We needed those jobs and knew that Carlton's reign over us would only last until the fire season's end. It was less that he hated the men working under him, and more that he didn't fully understand that for the majority it was a summer job and not a permanent way of life.

2018

My Challenging Bastard

A Bastard and Father moment on the Little Spokane Fire (2015).

Left to right: Chester (my bastard) and Me (his bastardly father)

Severe fluorescent light falls on the cool grey cement floor in the mess hall as Chester puts the bottle to his lips and tips his head back, the bottle up, It is June 2013, and out the window, the sky is fading blue to pink to black and ponderosa pines and fir trees brush the horizon, a green pelt of needles, soon night will come and the call of owls but now all to be heard is the glub glub glub of devil colored hot sauce emptying out of a quart sized glass bottle, Chester with the bottle in one hand, his Adam's apple pumping up and down chugging the liquid pain, Eric –

now mouth cocked open, he's staring holes through him, shaking his head from side to side.

Now the bottle is halfway empty, and I, too, stare in disbelief at Chester, for no more than sixty seconds ago that bottle of hot sauce had been new, full, sealed, and now there is maybe a half an inch left, as Chester yanks the bottle from his lips, slaps a hand over his mouth and bounds toward the 55 gallon plastic garbage can, gripping onto the outside handles and unleashing a torrent of red, rising up on his toes as he does so, the sound is that of two-hundred and fifty dollars reversing out of him and splattering on the floor of the empty garbage can.

He might have had the will to win; but he just didn't have the guts for it.

That's my first clear memory of Chester O'Reilly, also known as Chet, also known as My Bastard. It had been the first week of our rookie fire season, that first week with its days of endless orientations and training. I had, moments before, been in the mess hall making an after dinner snack when Chester and Eric entered – all youth and ignorance – when I overheard Chester boast of how he could down an entire quart of hot sauce in one go. Doubting Eric bet him a thousand dollars that he couldn't, with Chester then proving both his naïveté and innocence when he countered his offer, telling him, hubristically, in his rough and tobacco spattered voice, that he felt a thousand dollars was far too much for a feat he could easily accomplish, he'd settle for two-hundred and fifty instead.

Thus, the first of many of what became to be known as Chester Challenges was born.

He was (is) My Bastard. On our fire crew there was a saying, "there are no secrets on the Highlands 20," which meant there were no secrets to be had as we lived, worked, and played together for an entire summer and by the end there was no chance of keeping anything hidden. It should then come as no surprise that both the year I lost my virginity and the year that Chester was born was soon revealed to be one in the same, and from that day until our last, the running joke is that he was (is) my bastard son, and, I, his deadbeat bastard of a dad.

Chester. Nineteen. Bright-eyed. Likeable. Hardworking. Eager. Mutton chops. Rattlesnake tattoo on one arm, sprawling bald eagle tattoo on the upper half of his back, and the words: “Keep it Klassy,” yes, you read that correctly, classy with a “K” – in the font used by Keystone Light, his favorite beer – tattooed on his buttocks. If Chester had one downfall it was his mouth, as the brakes between it and his brain were thin. He’d often ask the wrong question at the wrong time to the wrong person about the wrong subject, usually that person was his squadboss, who would later pull me aside spitting tobacco juice and blinking in disbelief and tell me that the shit that flowed from Chester’s mouth made him think that in the nation of wildland firefighters, Chester didn’t have the brains to be on a fire engine, let alone a member of the Highlands 20. It was in these moments, these times of expressed doubt, that my nonexistent, yet invoked paternal instincts would emerge and I would stick up for my counterfeit bastard, telling him that what Chester lacked in smarts he made up for in strength, in spirit. Like any father would, I felt the judgment of my bastard was too harsh, because as far as I had observed brains were not a mandatory to be a wildland firefighter. It took a strong back. It took a willingness to put yourself in harm’s way. It took basic reading skills. And Chester had all of those, in spades. On top of all of that, all bastard jokes aside, Chester reminded me of myself at that age.

Our second wildfire of 2013 was a small and unnamed lightning strike of a fire that burned less than an acre in the mountains above our Fire Camp – the kind of fire that takes longer to hike into than it does to put out. After hiking miles up a steep forsaken slope, after digging fireline around the thunderbolt charred tree and surrounding terrain, after calling in a rotor (helicopter) to make a few bucket drops (of water) so we could mop it up, (a term that, oddly enough has nothing to do with mops and everything to do with making sure that a fire has zero chance of restarting once wildland firefighters leave an incident) it was then, as the sun was hot and the air was clear, as the Highlands 20 got off our feet and waited for the rotor to arrive, that the second Chester Challenge took place.

As any wildland firefighter who has battled blazes in the Pacific Northwest knows, there is a specific type of flying shit of a bug, known in firefighting circles as Stump Humpers, an invasive species that almost immediately exits burnt trees they have claimed as their home once a fire has been suppressed. These bugs look menacing - with their bodies the length and diameter of a man's pinky finger, their waxy wings, and their posteriors sharpened to a fine point – especially when they swarm around you. They won't sting, as what looks like a stinger is merely a protruding piece of their exoskeleton, but they will take sharp and painful bites out of any exposed flesh: face and neck and wrists.

I tell you about Stump Humpers, not to embellish or horrify, but to give you the subject of Chester's next stomach churning challenge. Being the industrious and adventurous young man that he is; he had a simple scheme in mind. He was going to eat a Stump Humper and charge the crew fifty dollars to witness his feat of gastrointestinal savagery, both to make money and to be accepted by the crew as "that wild and crazy guy who would do anything for a laugh," a mantle that most young men can relate to, or, at least, I did at his age.

His feat had only one flaw. No one cared. Realizing that no one wanted to pony up the cash to see him eat a bug, he quickly renegotiated his own proposal, announcing that he would do it for a 30 pack of Keystone Light, because, surely, the crew would pitch in for something they could all benefit from.

After capturing a Stump Humper that was crawling down his

sleeve, he stood before the gathered crew and wiped his mouth with the back of one hand, and held the insect between his thumb and pointer finger in the other, eying it nervously. He paused, brow beaded with sweat. We, the rest of the crew, circled round – phones and digital cameras at the ready. All eyes on Chester. The Stump Humper, sensing its demise, curled its body into a defensive position. His bug holding hand quivered. Through the mountains the faint chud-chud-chud-chuding echo of the rotor we'd radioed in grew louder. Chester looked from the squirming bug, to us: his crewmates, his face awash with dread.

I sensed that he was about to renege on his own challenge, so I began to count backwards from ten, aloud. For the uninitiated: there is something magical that happens in a young and impressionable males mind when he hears a countdown just before he's about to do something stupid or dangerous in front of a crowd. It somehow blocks out all recognition of their actions and gives them the courage to carry on, regardless of the outcome, because no one wants to be considered weak by their peers, especially if it was their own doing that got them in their current predicament.

Ten: Chester ran his tongue between his lower lip and his gum and spat out a wad of wet tobacco.

Nine: he clenched his jaw, no doubt his sphincter too, furiously shook his head from side-to-side, and began to inhale and exhale short and rapid breaths.

Eight: the Stump Humper, aware that a big smack-down was coming, squeezed and released its abdomen to its thorax, either in a vain attempt to free itself or one final tiny ab workout.

Seven: the sweat that beaded on his brow cascaded down his face, slopping off his chin in large visible drips.

Six: The chud-chud-chud-chuding of the rotor now sounded like thundering punches against the blue sky as it became visible, only a few more seconds till we'd be ordered back to work.

Five: Chester did not wait for zero. With a flick of the wrist he popped the Stump Humper into his mouth. Cameras clicked. We, the gathered crowd: whooped and hollered. His jaw moved fast and faster still. He swallowed hard. His Adam's apple struggled to get the mass of spiny bug parts down his throat. He urgently chugged water from his canteen then stuck out his tongue for inspection.

Chester – 1. Stump Humper – 0.

To no one but Chester's surprise, a 30-pack of Keystone Light was never purchased for completing his Stump Humper challenge. Because when it came down to it he was so excited to do something that would set him apart, make him liked by all, that he had thrown out terms for his challenge, but no one had actually agreed to them.

Sixteen years prior, in my economics class in high school, my teacher had the acronym: T.N.S.T.F.L. written on the chalkboard. When asked what it meant, he said, "There's no such thing as a free lunch." Obviously, he never anticipated that one Chester O'Reilly would prove him wrong.

I have a confession to make… I hate chewing tobacco. There, I said it. I always have and always will. There are men I know that those would be fighting words if said to their face. I, however, am not one of those kinds of men. I've just never found the appeal in loading my lips with something that is clearly trying to do me harm. Have you ever read the warning labels on those brightly colored paper pouches and plastic cans? They read like a hillbilly nightmare - gum disease, tooth loss, mouth cancer – and if you listen close you can almost make out a lone banjo in the background. It is not just the promise of a rotting mouth that turns me off, it's the endless spitters: plastic water bottles half-full of slimy brown tobacco saliva, it's the ribbons of brown spittle and chodes of nicotine glued to beards and splattered onto shirts – the hallmark of discharged tobacco that didn't hit the mark. I admit, I used to smoke cigarettes – from the age of sixteen to twenty-one - and if that makes me a hypocrite, so be it.

Yet in all my years of life, of all the careers and professions I've dabbled in, both blue and white collar alike, I have never come across so many people that chewed tobacco than when I fought wildfire. I'd estimate that 90% of the wildland firefighters that I have met and worked with have all chewed tobacco. I often wondered if the wildfire industry was singlehandedly keeping the chewing tobacco manufacturers afloat. It sure seemed that way. I recall that when en route to every fire that was more than a few minutes from our Fire Camp that the Highlands 20 would make special stops at the tobacco shack on the reservation to load up on can after can of tax free chew.

I've tried to like the stuff. Twice in my youth I was offered a chaw, and both times ended with me emptying my guts in less time than it took to read this sentence. If that makes me a weak specimen, I accept defeat. Some might say, "third times the charm." I rebut that with a resounding, "fuck off!" So it was with great glee and morbid fascination when Chester's next challenge came to be: The Great Chew-Off of 2013.

It began at the Clockum-Tarps Fire, on the drought-riddled mountains outside of Wenatchee, Washington, with their dry grass and empty skies. We waited for four days for the winds to be in our favor before we could begin a backburn, a tactic used to reduce fuels between wildland firefighters and the fire itself. During that 'hurry up and wait' period the Highlands 20 had little else to do than nap, read, and talk shit – which we excelled in. It was first introduced by the Cali Boys (Jimmy, Rich, and Andy) and began as a friendly contest between Taylor and Larsen and Chester to see who could keep a wad of chew in the longest, a way to kill time while we waited for our backburn. That 'friendly contest,' however, quickly escalated into a full on challenge of chewing prowess.

The challenge was thus: each of the men would empty an entire can of chewing tobacco into their mouths and wait ten minutes. The last one to keep the chew in the longest won a log (ten cans of chewing tobacco) of their choice. There was only one rule: if any man spat tobacco saliva during the event they would be disqualified. Simple. Easy. However, our overhead (crewboss and squadbosses) overheard the plans and wisely postponed the challenge until the Highlands 20 was off the Clockum-Tarps Fire and back at our Fire Camp in Loomis, Washington, because they knew far better than we that a challenge of this sort would be a stomach expelling riot and best done when not in the eyes of other fire crews.

Fourteen days later, after earning a singular 24-hours free from fire, an R&R day, our fire crew was at our summer home, the Highlands 20 Fire Camp.

We arrived “home” around 1300, and spent the next three and a half hours getting fire ready, a term that refers to being ready to roll out to a fire in a moments notice, which meant: chainsaw maintenance, tool maintenance, vehicle maintenance, filling out paperwork, and doing laundry. During which, Frank, our saw team leader, walked around with pen and pad taking bets on The Great Chew-Off of 2013.

1630. The afternoon was hot, the air dry. Tall pines spiked under the huge blue sky. On the edge of Fire Camp a doe and two spotted fawns grazed on unmowed grass. The crew was off the clock and after hearing our crewboss give us the 'don't get arrested or the local girls pregnant R&R speech' - which was always needed as when we'd come off of a fourteen day rotation from a fire that we'd spent miles upon miles hiking and cutting and digging fireline we'd be thinking of nothing but beer and sex - the twenty of us circled around the picnic tables in front of the office in anticipation of The Great Chew-Off of 2013.

The three challengers: Chester, Larsen, and Taylor posted up on the picnic tables; each held a sealed can of chewing tobacco in their hands. Last minute bets were placed. Larsen and Taylor were the crew favorites. Chester was the dark horse. No one believed in him, so no one betted on him. Hell, I didn't bet on him either, it wasn't because I didn't think he could win, quite the contrary, I knew he'd win, he was (is) my bastard after all. I didn't bet for the simple fact that I'm not a gambling man.

Frank shouted that betting was over.

Frank shouted for them to empty their entire cans into their mouths, which they did cramming every last shred of moist tobacco into their lips, cheeks, and under their tongues.

Frank shouted, "You got ten minutes! Go!"

For a brief speck in time the whitetail, which had been nonchalantly munching, looked up from the grass to our commotion.

Rabid curses were barked. Pictures were taken from every angle. The faces of the three contenders flushed red, from the rush of nicotine, from the hot blood boiling beneath their skin. Unable to spit the tobacco juice meant they had to swallow it, intensifying the effects of the nicotine in their bloodstream. Soon, their entire bodies began sweating uncontrollably. Their eyes glazed dazed, their mouths open like dirty shotgun wounds. Their breath quickened to the point of gasping.

Five minutes passed like this before Larsen, his body on the brink of uncontrollable spasms, leaned over the picnic table and loosed his guts onto the gravel. Taylor didn't look at Larsen; he didn't have to, the sound of his retch too much to bear. He cocked his head to the side of the picnic table and emancipated his nicotined mouth as well as the roast beef he'd had for lunch. Chester, unfazed by the others chunder, gave me, the only crewmember cheering him on, two thumbs up and a black hole grin.

I give him a half-smile and a thumbs up in return and hold two thoughts simultaneously in my mind as the crowd dissipates: Chester will finally be able to collect something tangible from his self-induced challenges, and what does the family of feeding deer think of us and our odd and sickening gathering? Neither thought stays for long as the smell of summer sweetness on the wind overtakes me, brings me back into the present. What exists for me is the pride in my longshot of a bastard and the foretaste of the ice-cold R&R beer to come.

A few weeks have passed since Chester won The Great Chew-Off and the Highlands 20 are now assigned to the Silver Star Fire, a name dripping with irony as there are neither silver nor stars to be seen, only the ashen landscape that looks to have been touched by the fourth horseman of the apocalypse: Death. I see grey. The color surrounds me for as far as sight will allow. My fire crew is lined out in a gridding pattern scouring this mesa of doom for any sign of heat, of smoke, of any remnant of flame that could bring back to life what is dead. There are no trees. There are the blackened skeletal remains of sagebrush clawing at the sky. There is the feeble and twisted sketch of barbwire one must be careful not to get tangled in. The air sags with dust and ash. A hard wind blows that same dust and ash into our grizzled faces. We grid from our buggies to the opposite side of this 75-acre fire. The fire was contained, stomped out, put to bed, removed from this plane of existence six days prior. This is our seventh day on the fire. This is a political fire.

A political fire, as I learned, is the name for fires that are suppressed but the powers that be keep resources (firefighters, fire engines, bulldozers, etc.) on them in order to make sure those resources are close at hand in case a new start rears its flaming head.

For six days we had crossed that hostile moonscape. For six days we monitored that suppressed fire, ensuring that no flame was left alive. For six days we had been given the same briefing at the start of each shift. We were warned of all manner of hazards – rattlesnakes, bees, cactus, barbwire, boredom, and the most dangerous of all: the evil eye of the all-seeing public.

Since the chance of a restart was nonexistent, we spent the first 30 minutes of each day gridding the dead earth, and the other 15 hours and 30 minutes of our days reading, napping, joking – things that had to be kept hidden from the public as they could, and never would, understand that though we worked for them, we were humans and not nonstop firefighting robots. We needed downtime. We needed to recuperate our strength. We needed to gather our fading wits. We needed to laugh and not be judged for it. We needed a political fire.

It was in this climate of secrecy that the last Chester Challenge of 2013 came to pass. While the crew was chasing shade, sleeping off that day's sack lunch in a clandestine meadow of thigh high sun dried grass the color of boot leather, Chester, unable to nap, and still riding the high of winning and collecting the spoils from The Great Chew-Off, wandered until he happened upon a prickly rose bush; it was there as he gazed upon its spiny limbs that he imagined his final challenge.

Thorn branch.

Bare ass.

Three hundred dollars.

After conspiring with Frank, the Highlands 20's resident bookie, the challenge was set. The crew would ante up three hundred dollars. Chester would bear his bare ass to all present. A spiky rose branch would be whipped across said, "bare ass," three times. Chester would collect three hundred dollars. Easy peasy.

Word of Chester's ass whipping spread like blood in the water, and all the sharks woke to get a taste. Money changed hands. Promises of IOU's were written, and kept. For less than sixteen dollars a head we were promised to see Chester in pain. No one could resist. I pitched in twenty-five dollars, under one condition: I got to execute the final lash of the thorny whip because I, too, was overcome by boredom, by bloodlust, by being able to exercise my newfound bastard parental rights of corporeal punishment.

In less time than it took the sun to glide an inch westward in the blue sky, the crew was worked up into frenzy. Expectations of suffering were high. Though the political fire was needed, it left a void where once there had been work, and we were ready to fill that void with Chester's screams.

It was time. Chester stood before the crew, exposing himself to God and country, and assumed a hands on knees position. The crew circled round with faces of jackals. Taunting. Laughing. Swearing. Frank selected the spikiest branch and whittled one end into a handle. He, along with Cody, and I, lined up – the designated hitters.

Jeff told everyone to pipe down, and then in a calm and firm voice he called in the hourly weather to dispatch over his handheld radio, as is standard operating procedure for fire crews to do, even on political fires. When dispatch replied, "Copy," the crew roared once again.

Chester clenched his jaw, white-knuckled his kneecaps, turned his head to Cody, and nodded. He was ready for the pain.

Cody took the first swing. It was a disappointment. He did not bring the pain. He lightly grazed Chester's right cheek. The crowd was not pleased. Profanity flew in Cody's direction. He smirked and pushed his glasses up the bridge of his nose.

Chester momentarily relaxed his jaw and let out a sigh of relief, before Cody passed the thorn branch to Frank.

Frank was known to stroll through the barracks at the Highlands 20 Fire Camp, the nights that we weren't fighting wildfire, and go from bunk to bunk seeking midnight drinking comrades. If you agreed and got out of bed he'd call you a man. If you rolled over and put your pillow over your head he called you a pussy. With this knowledge the crew knew that he wouldn't hold back.

Frank stood behind Chester. He pushed his hat up on his forehead and chuckled. The crew was salivating, wanting to get their three hundred dollars worth, and knowing that this was it, he was the one who will make Chester scream so loud they'd hear him in Seattle. Frank cocked the thorny branch above his head. The sun stared at Chester's white ass with a dead eye. Frank released with the speed of s striking pit viper…at the moment before impact he pulled back. The result: a smack that was slightly harder than the last, but not by much. That time the crowd was silent. Frank was our overhead and no one wanted to hurl curses his way.

Chester again released the tension from his body before

clenching up. The thorn covered lash was now in my hand.

I don't know for a fact, but I hazard to guess that Chester had some kind of deal worked out with Cody and Frank, some kind of a 'if you don't brutalize me, I'll give you a cut of the cash' kind of deal. No such deal was struck with me.

The brown grass stiff with summer sun crunched under my boots making it hard to find solid footing. It was afternoon, the air rich with drought and readiness, Chester's pants-less ass already red from the sun. I felt the weight of the branch in my hand and judged its length to be about as long as a man's arm, the thorns, each about a half-inch in length, studded the limb. I teased him with soft lullaby caresses – three - seven – eleven times - wanting to get my money's worth, not wanting Chester to anticipate when I would plant those thorns into him. The surrounding crew laughed. I lined up as if I was about to clobber a golf ball and raised my thorn-encrusted driver back behind my head. The crowd went silent, their lean and grime smeared faces collapsed, their mouths became hard lines. I swung with all my might. I made contact. The branch shattered. Thorns buried into flesh. Blood dripped from his

"Keep it Klassy" tattoo. The crew erupts into a chorus of cheers, satisfied.

Even now I hear their whoops and hollers, on another continent and years and years later, even as I tell you this.

2018

Seasonal Love

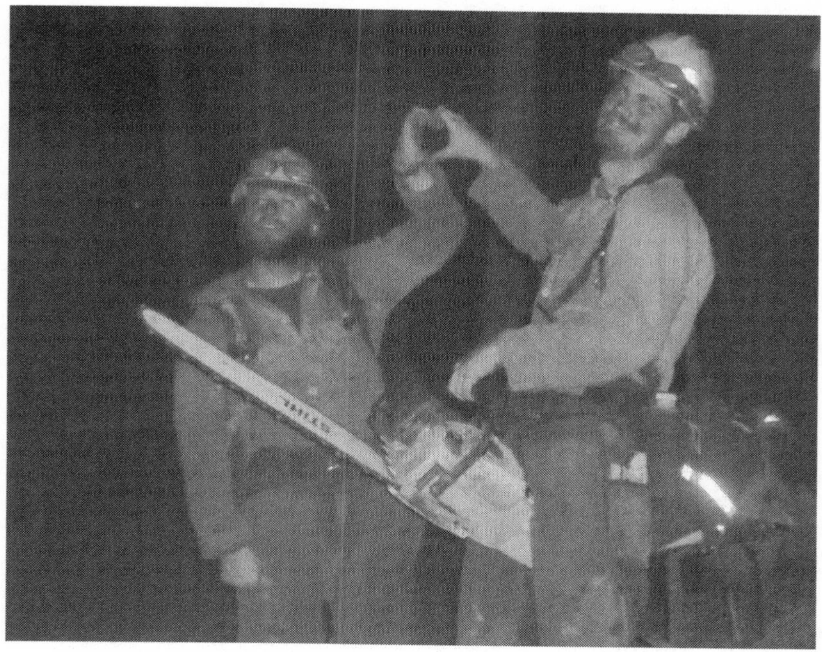

Squad One Saw Team showing some love on the Gold Hill Fire (2015). Left to right: Patty and Frenchie

This is an essay about relationships and wildland firefighting and it begins in Tonasket, Washington - less than a five-hour drive to Seattle, but it might as well be light-years away: not the Washington of rain-filled days and coasties and sophistication and culture, (fueled by the money of Amazon and Microsoft, all set to a soundtrack laced with prime cuts from Nirvana and Jimi Hendrix) but a rougher Washington, populated with men and women with callouses on their hands and chewing tobacco in their teeth, plunked right down in the high desert orchard heavy Okanogan County where musical tastes don't stray far from the country and western genre and anybody who is anybody drives a 4-wheel drive pickup truck. It is a town with a population of 1,017, a slice of living, breathing small town Americana – where you wave to people passing in cars because you know everybody and everybody knows you. A place where the air is clean, the water is safe to drink from the tap, the land is fertile, the winters are harsh and the only place hotter in the summertime is Hell.

It was in this unspoiled town where on the 19th of May 2014 a wife had a disturbing conversation with her husband. The wife in question was the Tonasket High School Librarian, a 37-year old medium build, shorthaired brunette, married for over a decade, and mother of two. She, under the duress of having her husband find out what she had done through channels of small town gossip rather than from her own lips, made a confession: she had been having an affair with a student. Her revelation, the stuff of bodice-ripping-chiseled-ab-Fabioesque romance novels, did not sit well with her husband, a man of action and of few words, who walked to their front yard, gun in hand; his entire world obliterated, he looked at the pistol - mulling over his options -

before raising it over his head and firing a single 9mm round into the air.

This was not an episode of a family drama, or an urban legend, or the opening scene from a three-act play about small town adultery. This incident involved Matt, my crewboss of three years on the Highlands 20, and his wife – who were both placed under arrest, he for discharging a firearm in public, and she for sexual misconduct with a minor. This took place three weeks before I was to begin my second fire season. Even though this emotional vignette could have ended far worse, it is emblematic of relationships with wildland firefighters.

Speaking of failed relationships and wildland firefighting it would be negligent of me not to mention my own. Mine was with Karalyn. We had had a whirlwind long distance relationship for a year – meeting on spring break in Venice Beach, spending a week of lust in Los Angeles in the fall, getting snowed-in together in New York over New Years Eve of 2014, going on a road trip down the entirety of the west coast, and capping off our year together with a week in Mexico before I began my second fire season. The day that I was to make my three-hour drive to the Highlands 20 Fire Camp I answered a phone call from Michigan. I can't remember the exact words that she spoke. I do remember that what she said was frank, curt, and earnest – three words that when used as names hold no meaning for me, but when used to describe our breakup tore my heart from my ribcage and stuffed the bleeding hole with a humungous shovelful of shit. Her breakup took me by surprise and added an emotional weight to my fire season. Heartache: one more thing for me to hump up the mountains. At least she was courteous enough to break up with me before fire season began, so that way I could go into the fray without any false hopes of a future together.

Such was not the case for my friend, Patty, during his rookie fire season. Patty – nineteen, EDM loving, and a self-proclaimed “giver” – had entered the 2013 fire season with his girlfriend of three years near and dear to his heart. She, however, did not see the benefit of waiting 90 days for him, and rather than break things off clean, she posted pictures of herself on social media that led one to believe that she was young, wild, and involved with someone else; shattering Patty’s heart in the process and leaving him with a month left on his contract to let his broken heart steep in the smoky broth of wildland firefighting. Which is both the best and worst place to experience heartache. It is the best place if you have a season that is ripping and you are so consumed with fire that you have no time to process the pain. In contrast, if you have a slow fire season where there are days, weeks, and sometimes, months between fires, it can be the worst place, as each day is a continual drag and a reminder that you chose to be there and while you are raking pine cones and choking back tears, she is at the lake in a bikini with all the guys back home who are 'just friends.'

*　　*　　*

Getting mail at the Highlands 20 Fire Camp was always a special occasion. We would be in the chow hall at the end of an in-camp shift (meaning that we had not been called to a fire), eating together as a crew on baby blue picnic tables when Don, our elderly camp cook's husband, would hand out the mail – the usual: letters and bills, but occasionally one of us would get a package, proving that someone in the 'real world' actually gave a damn. Those packages were almost always candy and books and other outdoors trinkets (pocketknives, flashlights, emergency blankets, etc.) that loved ones thought would make life more tolerable whilst we were fighting wildfire. There was one day in particular where one of us received a very special package.

Hambone got a box addressed from his friend in Olympia,

. It was the size of a shoebox, and, as was tradition, he ı for all to see the contents - a way to both show off what he had been sent and to make the rest of us wish someone we knew cared enough to send us something. He was talking as he ripped through the brown paper bag used to secure the package, not paying attention as he revealed to all in attendance, including Judy, our surrogate cigarette smoking grandma turned camp cook, the box for a male masturbatory aid; a rubber vagina. Judy's eyes widened, her jaw, slack in disbelief. The rest of us laughed our guts out. Hambone's eyes bulged. His face flushed - white to bubblegum pink. He quickly rewrapped the brown paper around the boxed pussy and hurried off to the barracks. He named her Fiona. He carried her in his linepack. She was low maintenance and never broke his heart.

* * *

Seasonal relationships seemed to be the norm in wildland firefighting. By relationship I do not mean the kind where you would take the other out to dinner, seduce them with words and wine, and get to know them in the hopes of finding someone compatible. No, these 'seasonal relationships,' were more of an exchange of bodily fluids and little else.

That is not to say they did not serve a purpose; mainly, to keep you from having so much sperm backed up in your brain that it clouded your decision-making, and most importantly, bragging rights.

On the first day of the 2014 fire season, the Highlands 20 sat beneath the towering pines of our Fire Camp with the rising sun filtering through the branches heating the earth around us, we picked bacon from our teeth and tried not to giggle at everyone's loud and rippling farts, all while Matt gave us our very first morning briefing of the summer, telling us the type of fire season he predicted and what he expected from us, it was then that a Washington State Department of Fish and Wildlife vehicle rolled into our parking lot. This was common as our Fire Camp shared resources and facilities with Fish and Wildlife. What was not common was who exited the vehicle. Amber – female, 21, perky, pretty – she smiled an effervescent smile at nineteen wolfish faces (Matt had his back turned to her) that licked their chops and undressed her with their eyes as she drifted like cotton candy on a warm summer breeze from her vehicle and into an out-building.

Amber was an anomaly. First, she was an attractive female, which if you have ever traveled to North Central Washington you will understand that alluring women are as common as it snowing in July. Second, she was single. It was the standard in that area that if there was a beautiful woman she would be tied down with either a wedding ring or a child, because in small towns and rural areas across America, the best way to ensure someone stays is to either marry them or fill them with child. Finally, she was, as Patty would say, "a giver." By the seasons end she had given herself to 20% of the Highlands 20. I have no doubt that had the opportunity presented itself that she would have given herself to all 20 of us, but there were those of us who knew what dirty bastards we were and did not want to take the chance of becoming tainted tunnel buddies. That being said, it was probably the most copacetic fire season relationship (human-to-human, that is), as all parties involved walked away smiling.

* * *

20 August 2015: It was the Highlands 20's last day on the Gold Hill Fire. Six days prior we had been first responders. Chaos ruled the scene. A civilian had died trying to evacuate. Resources were nonexistent. For a fire that was eating acres of timber at an alarming rate there were only two fire engines and we, the Highlands 20. We stomped up the extreme

incline, dug fireline around the blaze, and set fire to the rest – back-burning all the remaining fuel, and though the fire was suppressed, it was not out. However, it was our fourteenth consecutive day on fire, which meant it was our final day before we timed out, before we were to take a mandatory R&R day.

Chester and I stood on the fireline leaning on our tools, our eyes to the green, the unburnt area, while behind us Javi flung fire from a driptorch. As the flames grew larger and demonically devoured the fuel separating us from the head of the fire, we planned for our sacred 24-hours away from the crew. While I was outlining every sordid detail of the hotel rendezvous I was planning to have with a woman I had met on Tinder, Chester was unsure what he should do. He told me that he was in love with a female friend back in Ellensburg. He said they had always been friends and asked if I thought he should express his love to her.

At that moment I felt like I had accomplished something. Someone looked up to me enough, to not only ask for my counsel, but I knew that they would act upon it. I regurgitated all the advice I had been given throughout my life, I told him, "Fortune favors the bold," and "If you don't ask then the answer is always 'no'," and my favorite,

“A closed mouth don’t get fed.” I told him that he should definitely tell her how he feels, empty the contents of his heart. What’s the worst that could happen?

48 hours later, after our R&R day, after the Highlands 20 had reunited, after I had gone on an odyssey through road blocks and fields on fire and witnessed a legion of animals running away from a wall of flames as if it were the end of days, after I had spent a passionate and pleasure-filled time with my Tinder match, yet before my hangover had wormed its way out of my brain, I reconnected with Chester. It was then that I found out the worst that could happen.

The cavalier guidance I had given him was based upon a three things. (1) I had previously seen the two of them together and when around one another, they lit up, becoming noticeably brighter in each other’s presence. (2) Chester had always talked about her with reverence, which meant that he respected her, and that was a good and rare thing. (3) 2015 was a dangerously intense fire season, and I thought, that at the very least even if she didn’t have feelings for him she would want to have sex with him for the fact that he had been risking his life for the betterment of mankind.

I was wrong.

While my hotel rendezvous had been a bit of seasonal love, Chester's R&R day had been peppered with disappointment. He had followed his plan to the letter. He asked her over to his place. He opened a bottle of wine. He made her dinner. He looked deep into her eyes and courageously shared his heart with her, confessing that he was not only her friend, but also that he had harbored romantic feelings for her for a long time. He did all the things that he had seen done to successfully woo a woman on the silver screen. He, however, was not met with teary eyes and passionate kisses, but silence. She left, telling him that she needed to process all he had said. He told me this as we filled our CamelBaks and readied our linepacks for another sixteen-hour shift.

One long week later he received a text from her. We were parked in his car a few miles from our Fire Camp, the closest place we could get cell service. And since there are no secrets on the Highlands 20, Chester let me read what she had written. It was a long and rambling text that I can sum up in these few words - thanks, but no thanks. He asked me what I thought he should reply, but it was too late.

I had already replied for him.

Just one word...

Poop.

*   *   *

Why is it that love is so difficult to find and hold onto for wildland firefighters? Is it the long hours and time away from home? Is it that wildland firefighters give so much whilst on the job that they are spent (physically and emotionally) when they return home? Is it that the thrill of the job is more interesting than the minutia of a relationship? Why have 99% of all the wildland firefighters that I've known either been single, divorced, or in toxic relationships? My hunch is that most wildland firefighters are just plain hard to get along with in 'normal life,' and that it's not the fire season that kills relationships, but the off-seasons when they spend more time with their significant other and not in the company of fellow wildland firefighters. I once read that the "divorce rate for firefighters is three times that of the general population..." If that is the case and the divorce rate of America in 2017 was 36% that would mean that 108% of firefighter marriages end in divorce. Those are not good odds.

And if an almost-guaranteed-divorce is the rule with the marriages of wildland firefighters, then there must be exceptions to the rule, those statistical flukes that have slipped through the cracks of dissolution and remained intact. Out of my four years of wildland firefighting and the dozens of firefighters I worked and became friends with there was only one whom I know that has stuck with both the vocation and his marriage.

Billy, a Tonasket native and son of an orchardist, had gotten married one week before I started my rookie fire season (2013). Mild temperament. Ever-present smile. Slow to anger. Quick to laugh. Billy was 24 at the time. I recall driving our squad's buggy back from the Rattlesnake Fire as he rode shotgun. At the time I could not believe that a man so young, with a college education and a bright future with endless possibilities would settle down with a girl from his hometown. It seemed idiotic to me and I told him so. He took my criticism of his life choices with a flash of a grin and a raise of his eyebrows; I'm sure he was thinking that I was just as nuts for being single in my mid-thirties. And yet he backed the right horse.

This essay concludes in the same high desert small American

town in which it began – Tonasket, Washington - more accurately, a few miles south of town at an apple orchard along the banks of the Okanogan River. It was there at a barbecue that I met Billy's wife later in the season, and saw the two of them interact and it all made sense. Though I was 34 at the time I had never known the kind of love that they felt for one another. They gave each other soft glances and stole kisses when they thought no one was looking. Though the crowd that was gathered was rowdy and cursed loudly and scarfed Jell-O shots and drank beer as if our very lives depended on it, the two of them were in *our* world but not *of* our world. Together they seemed somehow elevated and I admired Billy for that. For theirs was not a seasonal love but a love for all seasons.

2018

The Boys of Summer

"Camaraderie: a spirit of familiarity and trust existing between friends"

Squad One on the Enterprise Fire (2014) From left to right: Angel, Gonzalez, Nick, Patty, Frenchie, Charles (me), and Larsen

1.

In the summer of 2013 I was thirty-four, and I lived from June through September at the Highlands 20 Fire Camp outside of Loomis, Washington (more accurately: the-middle-of-nowhere-Washington). It was a perfect summer, as far as fire seasons are concerned; an equal balance of work and party, and the best summer of my life. Not because I made more money than the pope or I got laid all summer long or I spent it on a yacht drinking champagne, sailing the royal blue waters of St. Tropez. No, it was the best summer of my life because by summer's end I had gained something I had never had before – fire brothers.

Fire Camp was a special place unlike anywhere I have ever been. It was rural, remote, far from the beguilement of cellphone service or the World Wide Web. It suggested another world, another time, a world that was long gone, a world which now seems so far removed from the collective consciousness that it is even hard to imagine that a world like that ever existed: a man's world. It was a land void of women where political correctness had not tainted the mindset, a place where a man could piss wherever he pulled his dick out, could curse and be rude and say things that would make his mother want to wash his mouth out with soap and no one even blinked an eye. There, sun seared flesh, terrain was unforgiving, lakes blue and beer cold. You were respected for your hard work and expected to work hard. It was a place where you could grow a bushy mustache or a scraggly beard or shave your head or have a mullet all without the stigma of what society deemed unfashionable. At Fire Camp you worked, played, ate, slept, and showered side-by-side with the same 20 men for the duration of the fire season – which made the crew proverb, "There are no secrets on the Highlands 20," even more relevant. It was a place for men who wanted to be men and be in the company of likeminded men. There, we sharpened our chainsaws and oiled our boots and hiked the surrounding mountains in preparation for our next bout with Nature. We argued about real boobs versus fake tits, how Washington 10s were, at most, Cali 7s, why chewing tobacco was more disgusting than smoking cigarettes. Fire Camp was a world of loyalties and ball breaking, of strength over weakness and shared cigars, drunken nights and blistered feet and skinning rattlesnakes, a place where we shared our most intimate secrets and played pranks and talked about all the pussy we were going to get when what we really wanted was love. Despite the filth that ran through our thoughts and poured from our mouths, being removed from civilization as we were somehow made us innocent again. It acted as a portal that transported us from the dimension of nightly news, stock market debacles, social media, and racial and sexual tensions, to a simpler reality; one in which all that mattered was keeping each other safe and alive and going home in one piece at the day's end. In Fire Camp, it mattered not how difficult the situation was, you adhered to a

Code of manliness, which was thus: Don't be a pussy. We were the Lost Boys of our very own Neverland. We were a tribe. Fire Camp was Eden lost.

However, Fire Camp was just a physical locale, while it was us, the crew of the Highlands 20 that made Fire Camp what it was, gave it its soul. We were an island of men in a sea of fire.

Being a wildland firefighter was not all ball-breaking and having a few laughs. No, we actually had to fight fire. The beauty of wildland firefighting was found in the physical act of fighting fire itself; by doing so it allowed us to shed all responsibilities, all cares, all external real world happenings, all beliefs and differences and focus on one goal: suppressing the fire by whatever means necessary. It was through that taxing act that we formed our strongest bond. We hiked into every fire in single file STO (Standard Tool Order), led by a squadboss, followed by the sawyers (chainsaw operators) and swampers (assistants to the sawyers) and the rest of the tools (Pulaskis, Rhinos, etc.). As you did so you kept your head down and focused your gaze on the heels of the man in front of you. Rarely anyone spoke. If they did it was a curse word. What was normal was to hear the labored breaths of those around you as you pounded your way step-by-step up the mountain. Every time you heard the lungs of your crewmates straining for air you felt a sense of solidarity. You were not alone in your misery.

That feeling of solidarity was even more intensified when we would reach a fire and begin to work, a unit of men that moved as one. We knew how to proceed, knew our tools, knew our job. No man wandered off or kicked back in the shade. When we hit the fire, it was 'go time.' Adrenaline that was already flowing then blasted through us. The flames. The heat. The smoke. The jet engine like roar of trees being eaten alive by wildfire while orders were shouted and chainsaws barked to life and the earth being severed by tools and rotors (helicopters) chud-chud-chud-chudding through the sky and the crackle of handheld radio chatter all culminated into a feeling of oneness. A oneness, that, as I was told, was only comparable to that of being in a combat situation.

And when the fire was contained and our buggy was once again parked at Fire Camp and the beer flowed in place of adrenaline and we wore our 'going to town clothes' and we flirted with the prettiest waitress in Okanogan County at the only decent place to eat in all of

North Central Washington, and we talked shit and railed each other and relived in words the fire we had just fought and felt blessed to be sitting down in air conditioning giving our blisters a much needed break, it was then, after all we had accomplished and all we had been through together that further cemented our unity.

2.

Though each of us had applied to the Highlands 20 of our own volition, it felt as if we had involuntarily given ourselves to a social experiment. One in which the removing of 20 men from the rest of the world and placing them in a dynamic and high stress environment would be analyzed and written about in textbooks.

One effect of our isolation was that we became territorial to the extreme. When on fires that had more than one fire crew, which was the majority of the fires that we fought, we worked with Smokejumpers, Hotshots and various other fire crews whether they were Feds, State, contractors, or con-crews (inmates trained to fight wildfire). Each time we did so we took a little more pride in who we were - we sucked in our stomachs and puffed out our chests. We looked down at every other fire crew and judged them accordingly. No matter how big their beards were or how filthy their Nomex, other fire crews were always viewed as weaker than we were. It was nothing short of a dick-measuring contest and we deemed ourselves to be the biggest cocks on the block. Though we did not always get along or even like every man on our own fire crew, when in the company of 'others' our tribe grew tighter because outsiders were seen as rivals, enemies. It was never verbally expressed by our overhead (crewboss and squadbosses), but, we, the Highlands 20, felt it and knew it. We had something to prove, if only to ourselves, that our crew was tougher, dirtier, and manlier than they were.

3.

During my three fire seasons spent on the Highlands 20 there were no females on the crew. That does mean that the Highlands 20 did not have women pre or post my tenure, but while I was there, there were none. The reason behind that decision was never disclosed but that did not stop the rumor train. If anything it only made it careen faster down the tracks. Rumors ranged from my crewboss' dislike for females in hardcore labor-intensive environments, to no females applying for the crew, to the females that did apply - not showing up for their interviews.

To say that the Highlands 20 was a misogynistic 'boys club' - the wildland firefighting equivalent of the *Little Rascals'* 'He-Man Woman Haters Club' - is only a half-truth. Yes, we were a boys club. There is no denying that. But we were not misogynistic, in fact: quite the opposite. We loved women and being away from them for as long as we were only strengthened our love and respect for the female population. Of course we talked about sex, you would be fooling yourself if you think that 20 red-blooded-American-men separated from women for months on end wouldn't, but despite that; our forced segregation made us miss more than just their reproductive parts. We missed their conversation, their sensibility, their laughter, their delicate scent, their soft touches and knowing glances, and most of all: their God given feminine essence that was missing in our penile clan. I once asked Carlton, Squad Two's squadboss, if there was an all-female equivalent of the Highlands 20. He spat a stripe of brown tobacco spit between his boots and replied, "You boys ***are*** the all-female equivalent of the Highlands 20."

There were times, however, that having no females on our crew was a liability. I recall two fires in particular; that if the females in question had not have had such pleasant personalities and understood that we were a bunch of pent up savages on the verge of a horny-mental-breakdown that we would have been booted off those fires immediately.

July 5, 2013: the Highlands 20 was assigned to the Rattlesnake Fire. We left our Fire Camp early in the morning as the steely sun jabbed streaks of yellow light across the high desert landscape, and made the three-hour journey to the Mt. Tolman Fire Center outside of Keller, Washington – a staging area for resources to gather as more information about the fire was being collected, assessed, and plans of attack drawn up.

Our anticipation of fighting wildfire was at an explosive point. With over half of the crew being rookies, we had spent hours and hours learning about fire through courses and bookwork but had never actually set foot on one. We were also about to explode for another reason: the crew had been separated from society, more importantly, from women, for one month at that point. Upon reaching the Mt. Tolman Fire Center our squadbosses told us to stay put inside the buggies while they checked us into the fire and got briefed on the situation and our mission.

Squad One, my squad, did as was told and sat in our buggy. We were on edge and talked shit, as usual, to pass the time and keep our minds off the unknowns of the fire that we were about to fight. Outside, two female wildland firefighters dressed in crew t-shirts and Greens (fire retardant pants) strolled by. Greens are not flattering on anyone who wears them, meant to be functional not fashionable, but to us, the two women appeared as goddesses in their baggy pants and loose fitting shirts. The seven of us stopped talking, and stared from our windows, leaning on each other's shoulders, leering like racy caricatures of randy men: eyes bulged, tongues unraveled from our slobbering mouths, peckers swelled to cartoonish sizes.

Rich, unable to control himself, yelled, "Fire hotties!"

The lady firefighters took it in stride and kept walking. My guess is one of two things happened: they either did not hear his verbal ejaculation, which I doubt because our windows were down and there were no other competing sounds, or they brushed it off as a 'boys will be boys' kind of catcall compliment. Did they ever know how much the seven of us lusted after them in that moment? They were so close, yet so far away.

One year later, the Highlands 20 was assigned to the Devil's Elbow Complex – a wildfire that raged on the Colville Indian Reservation. After a sixteen-hour shift our fire crew was at the ICP (Incident Command Post – a mobile basecamp that is setup on larger fires to support wildland firefighters with meals, showers, basic logistics, etc.) in Nespelem, Washington.

While we readied our tools and linepacks (a type of specialized backpack unique to wildland firefighting due to its weight distribution capability) for the next day on the fire, Larsen, my sawyer, sharpened and cleaned his chainsaw. He had removed the front cover and as he looked at all the bar oil and wood chips and blackened muck that had gotten caught in the interior of the saw he let out a sultry whistle, and said, "Oh, look at you, you *are* a dirty girl." At that exact moment a female EMT was passing by, upon hearing the whistle, and what could have been construed as a lewd comment, she whipped her head around – face pinched tight, eyes seeking the culprit. When she saw Larsen hunched over his chainsaw whispering sweet nothings to it, she gave a sympathetic glance - her eyebrows pushed upward together, her mouth melted into a slight smile – and kept walking.

Regardless of those few cheeky instances, having no females on the Highlands 20 was a good thing, as when being separated from anything in life that you take for granted it gives you a deeper gratitude for it. Whether its health, money, love – or in our case, women – it is only when it's far out of reach that you understand its genuine value.

Our sexual segregation also made us recall our every interaction we had had with the opposite sex. It was my experience on the Highlands 20 that 90% of all of our conversations were on the subject of women, and only 10% were on fire. As such, we analyzed, discussed, and talked about every aspect of our relations with females – from conversations we had had with them, to our regrets, to heartaches, and, of course, our conquests.

In retrospect, I feel I understand my crewboss' not wanting to hire women. It is not that he hated them or didn't think they could work as hard as men. Consciously or not, I feel that he wanted to transfigure our sexual energy into fierceness for firefighting. Did that work? I would have to say, yes. I worked harder and longer on the Highlands 20 –

sixteen hour days, for fourteen days at a time, sometimes back-to-back-to-back-to-back rotations – than I have elsewhere, before or since. But at what price? Yes, we were successful at making wildfire submit to our will, but by a fire season's end, we were nothing short of barbarians that were then loosed upon the world.

4.

Facial hair was a staple on the Highlands 20. It didn't matter if you only grew a few sprigs on your upper lip or your face resembled a furry shrub. Everyone stopped shaving. There were numerous reasons why. Foremost was laziness, or as I like to call it: conservation of one's power. Wildland Firefighting requires mass amounts of energy, therefore, when not fighting fire you try to conserve that energy, and shaving, once you realized was done for beautifying rather than out of necessity, went by the wayside.

Superstition was another factor. Wildland firefighters are a superstitious lot, and unlike the general public, each summer they pray to the fire gods for the world to burn. This was done because all the flames and chaos and destruction, though recognized as negatives, were also seen as the way to pay the bills. That being the case, one of the superstitions that were supposed to appease the fire gods, a not very demanding bunch of deities, was to stop shaving for the duration of a fire season. It was always a disappointment when someone broke that unwritten commandment and came to morning briefing clean-shaven - especially if their transgression was followed by a fire-less few days, sometimes weeks.

Another reason was the fabled: Stachetember. The logic behind that was never made clear, other than it was supposedly a month likened to Movember, an annual event meant to raise awareness about men's health issues through the growing of a mustache. Though, I never have nor will understand how wanting to have a hair covered upper lip makes one think of prostate cancer. Stachetember was just an excuse for us to grow mustaches, plain and simple.

There was another underlying impetus behind all of these. It was one more way to proclaim that we were part of a tribe that was bigger than ourselves, it was in our blood, in our XY chromosomes, it sprang from our testosterone-filled-loins and cried to us from the past – we were men and this was our statement to the rest of the world of who we were, of our manhood, of our brotherhood. This expression of our genetic birthright was confirmed when we would venture out beyond the borders of our Fire Camp to ICPs across the state. There we would see that we were not alone. There were others like us; others that had foregone a razor's steel, who grew beards and mustaches as badges of pride.

One early August day of 2013, the Highlands 20 was assigned to the Clockum Tarps Fire on the outskirts of Wenatchee, Washington. We worked side-by-side with the Rogue River Hotshots – each of them seemingly over 6ft. tall, muscular, and with glorious facial hair (minus the women, though it wouldn't have surprised me if they had had mustaches too). Of course we reckoned that we were stronger than they were, as conceding defeat was never an option, but we did marvel at their facial hair. With our first attempts sprouting from our faces like baby spinach, we appreciated the time, effort, and devotion that had gone into their full-blown 'man gardens.'

Our two fire crews backburned that day, meaning: that we burnt the fuel (trees, grass, brush, etc.) between the fire, and us, in the hopes of stopping it in its tracks. As burners were given driptorches and began to drop fire, the rest of us stood on the fireline with our eyes on the green (the unburnt area) to ensure that no spot fires (unexpected fires in the green) occurred. We were positioned on the fireline one Hotshot, one of us, one Hotshot, one of us, so on and so forth - with 50ft. between each man. Close enough to see each other, but far enough away to keep conversations to a minimum.

I stood at one end of the fireline – back straight, muscles tensed, game face on – wanting to make a solid impression on the Hotshot to my right. He, however, knew far better than I did that the posture one should take when holding the line should be one of comfort rather than of implied intensity. He packed his lower lip with tobacco. He put on mirrored aviator sunglasses. He leaned on his tool. After a few hours of standing and watching the green, losing myself in thought, I glanced over at the Hotshot and saw one of the coolest maneuvers I've ever seen in my life. In the most nonchalant way, he removed a plastic comb from his chest pocket and began combing his burly mustache.

Soon thereafter, I, too, bought a comb and began running it through my beard and mustache. The rest of the Highlands 20 followed suit. From then on it was the one grooming device that each of us carried at all times. Whatever fire we were on, whatever ICP we camped at, our crew could be seen - comb in hand - smoothing out our spiny facial hair. I often wonder if that Hotshot knows the impact that he had on 20 men from Washington State?

I had never grown facial hair until I fought fire. I was 34 and was not even aware that I could produce more than slight fuzz. I mean, technically, I knew that I could, but I had always shaved it off after a few days as it looked patchy and silly. It wasn't until I had stopped shaving for weeks at a time, letting all the gaps fill in that I realized that it was possible for me to cultivate a beard that I could be proud of. Which, as I found out, was the case for most of the men on my fire crew. Together, we explored this new frontier of ourselves and discovered what each of us was capable of achieving.

Larsen could grow no more than a neard (neck beard) and chinstrap, which gave him an Amish-like appearance. Jeff was blessed with a thick, bristly Tom Selleck mustache. Andy's ginger goatee gave him the appearance of a cartoon mouse. While Valle's wiry beard, after being trimmed down to a mustache, made him look like Wario, Super Mario's arch-rival. Warner was notorious for his goat (chin beard) without the tee (mustache). Patty's facial hair was a lesson in evolution. In his rookie fire season it was little more than sparse areas of lint but by his third year it had blossomed into a thicket of dirty wool. My attempt at facial hair proved that I could grow a beard, not a thick one, but a beard I was satisfied with.

Through our experimentations of masculine expression we came to know ourselves, and each other, better than we had before. On R&R days we traded grooming tips and passed around scissors, razors, and clippers. We praised those whose outcroppings were bountiful and heckled the rest. We laughed at hipsters with their waxed mustaches and glittered beards – and became possessive of facial hair as if we owned the patent to it. We joked about how facial hair should only be grown by men who had earned the right to – wildland firefighters, policemen, Special Forces operators – men who put their lives on the line for their vocation. But behind that narrow-minded train of thought there was a pebble of truth, because for us, our facial hair was just as important as our boots, helmets, and Nomex. It was the spear tip of our identities, an outward expression of sacrifice and inner strength.

5.

When one thinks of wildland firefighting, or forest fires in general, numerous images come to mind: weary John Wayne-esque men in faded yellow shirts with sweat-ash-dirt-covered faces and crusty beards, or tall and imposing mountains destructively alive with red-yellow flames, or black plumes of smoke that strangle the blue sky and turn the sun the color of Armageddon, or planes skimming treetops opening their bellies to paint the fire with colorful retardant, or possibly one's mind goes back to childhood and *Bambi* as he raced through the forest, fire nipping at his hooves. What one does not think of are the vehicles that haul wildland firefighters to the fire itself, for it is in and around those man-haulers that we spent a majority of our time and bonded.

Speaking of bonding and buggies, it was at the start of each shift on a fire while we were around our buggies strapping on our linepacks and readying our tools that we performed what I termed a "Bonding ritual." Wildland firefighting is a strenuous job as such one sweats almost continuously out of every pore. And as anyone who has worked a job where sweat is a mainstay knows, one of the worst discomforts you can experience - colloquially known as "gig butt" or "monkey butt"

– is chafing in your nether regions. The "Bonding ritual" consisted of each of us passing around a shared bottle of Gold Bond, squeezing out a handful of the powder and applying it liberally to our backsides, front sides, and undercarriages; and whereas we were already perspiring the mentholated powder gave us a moment of respite that was reflected in a collective sigh. Frank, our saw team leader, put it best. "Gold Bond is like having a thousand ice fairies nibbling on your balls."

Sleeping was a favorite pastime. A typical day for the Highlands 20, when fighting fire, began at 0530, with breakfast at 0600, immediately followed by briefing (attended by the overhead) and preparation for that day's fire operations (performed by the rest of the crew which included: buggy checks [fuel, oil, windows, tires, lights], water and Gatorade procurement, gathering lunches, saw maintenance and tool sharpening). We were in transit to the fire by 0800. Usually on the fire by 0900 where work began, ending at 1900 when we would load up and be back at basecamp by 2000, prep for the next day until 2100, then dinner and off the clock by 2200. Needless to say sleep was a valued commodity and you slept whenever, wherever, and however you could.

In the buggy you learned to sleep through all the things that would have kept you wide awake in the 'real' world: light, bowel jostling roads, noise, foul odors (soul-searing farts and Nomex shirts – soiled with sweat and cardboard stiff), and being in too-close-for-comfort-proximity to males you were not related to. The social norm of personal space did not exist in the buggy. To fall asleep with your head on your seatmates shoulder and not think anything of it, or to be the owner of said shoulder, was commonplace. It gave a literal meaning to the Bill Withers song, *Lean on Me*. No one thought anything of it because over the course of a fire season you got to know your crewmates so well that they were no longer separate entities, but an extension of yourself.

Singing. Another prevalent yet overlooked aspect of wildland firefighting that was good for both coming together as one and morale. Of course music unites people; that is obvious – from church choirs to heavy metal concerts – music is a common front that likeminded individuals can agree upon. To think that wildland firefighters would be any different is absurd. When I was a crewmember of the Highlands 20 we prided ourselves in being a rowdy, loud-mouthed, work-hard-party-harder crew. The rowdy, loudmouth, party hard aspects were never more apparent on the job than when we would sing in our buggies. We sang to get psyched to fight fire – each song became our battle cry. We sang to celebrate leaving a fire – living to the end of another day. We sang to boost our spirits – the lyrics acted as balm to our over-masculinized selves. We sang to express our longings - to remind ourselves on those days without end that we had souls and were not just mindless beasts of burden.

People usually guess that we sang fire related songs, heavy metal songs with 'Fire' in the title. That couldn't be further from the truth. Our two go-to songs were: The Lumineers – *Stubborn Love*, and Journey – *Don't Stop Believing*.

Stubborn Love, though not rhythm heavy or bass pounding was sung at least once every time we sat in the buggy. There is nothing as unintentionally poetic as eight soot-soiled-bone-tired men putting everything they have into a song about lost love while racing to a burning forest.

Don't Stop Believing was my song, the song that I sang to my squad. The first time I did so was on a three-hour drive back to ICP. My squad was feeling blue and in need of a shot of positive energy so I played that Journey song on the Bluetooth speaker in the back of the buggy, jumped from my seat, using a broom as a make believe microphone, and began belting out the lyrics, hitting every nuance of every note. My captive audience did not disappoint. They cheered me on and shouted out the lyrics. Suddenly our buggy came to a bumpy halt. Within seconds the door to the buggy was jerked open. Our squadboss stepped into the back of the buggy, eyebrows knotted together, his mouth as tight as a bead weld, and asked what the hell was going on? He thought he had heard screams of pain and when he was unable to rouse us on the handheld radio he stopped to make sure that we weren't killing each other. Me, I still stood broom in hand. When I explained my impromptu karaoke session, we were told not to sing any longer, as wildland firefighters were not to give the impression to the ever-present eye of the public that, we, even in a remote way, were having a good time. He told us to nod our heads if we understood. Each of us nodded our heads in agreeance and crossed our fingers in defiance.

To me, crew morale and crew cohesion fed off of one another. In order for a crew to coalesce their self-esteem had to be high. At least, I thought it made sense. Therefore, as the senior most member of my squad (not counting my squadboss, who was one year older) I took it upon myself to do whatever I could to boost every man's ego, not to overly or falsely inflate it, but to point out their strengths and (hopefully) give them something to be proud of. I did this through giving speeches. To be fair, I only gave speeches to my squad, as they were the men I that knew best and worked with the most. After every fourteen-day rotation while our buggy was toting us back to the Highlands 20 Fire Camp I'd kill the music, stand up from my seat in the back of the buggy and go from man-to-man and give them compliments. I can't say if my armchair motivational speeches helped their performance as wildland firefighters, but it certainly made our squad tighter. I know this because my squadboss told me that he had never seen a squad grow as close as we had as fast as we had in all his thirteen years on the Highlands 20.

When we were fire bound we'd drive at breakneck speeds and bend traffic laws (never breaking them) to get to the incident. What this translates to is: that we would only stop if it were an actual emergency. That being said, we, in the back of the buggies, had to be fire-ready when we arrived on scene and able to jump out, gear up, and hike into the fire within minutes. Being Fire-ready meant not only having our linepacks and tools ready, it meant being mentally prepared, it meant having a full stomach, it meant being hydrated – because the foe of every wildland firefighter is dehydration.

To combat dehydration we would drink as much fluids (water and Gatorade) as we could en route to an incident. It was typical to put down a half gallon of fluids, or more, depending on how far the drive was. And as we all know what goes in must come out. Yet without the luxury of pulling over or having a urinal onboard we had to relieve ourselves in the buggy, into Gatorade bottles (the only bottles with mouths big enough to put your penis into) in the presence of our squad, which just hammered home the crew motto – "There are no secrets on the Highlands 20."

Q: What if you had a shy bladder? You know, stage fright, then what?

> A: You simply drank fluids until you were so overly hydrated that the thought of being bashful never crossed your mind because it took every ounce of grit you had not to piss yourself.

6.

Fire Camp was not for the shy. There you saw everyone naked at least once. Such are the pitfalls of showering together high-school-locker-room-style. You just trained your eyes not look down and tried to get in and out as quick as possible. No one ever wanted their crewmates to purposefully see their dick, except for Gonzalez who would expose himself on the regular just to get a laugh.

To help cut the tension of showering with your coworkers, Bluetooth speakers were brought into the latrine, and pretty soon we had what we dubbed Highlands 20 shower parties. It was never really a party, just a bunch of naked firefighters singing in the showers. I admit that it paints an unexpected and homoerotic picture of wildland firefighters, but; such is life. It did happen and it not only made our crew motto “There are no secrets on the Highlands 20,” even more true, there is no bonding experience quite like being threadbare and soaped up with your buddies singing along to *Friends in Low Places*.

7.

Outside of our Fire Camp, meaning: when the Highlands 20 was out fighting wildfires, and we camped either on the fireline or at an ICP, we found a skewed sense of satisfaction in being dirty – at seeing one's bright and pliable Yellow (fire retardant shirt) fade over the course of a fire season to a dingy-greyish-brownish color, crusted with salty sweat and peppered with ash, smoke, and dirt. It made us feel tough. We equated filth with masculinity. It was one more thing that separated us, the strong, from the rest of society, the weak. We were the lions. They were the lambs. We reveled in our dirtiness, drew strength from it, like a gang of filthy Samsons.

Despite the uncanny joy that I received from wearing a soiled Yellow I was a zealot about showering and wearing clean underwear and socks when on fires. I suppose my hypocrisy knows no bounds. It was one thing for me to be dirty but something entirely different to *sleep* dirty. Wildland firefighting is a filthy job, and I didn't mind getting dirty - the sweat, the smoke, the soot, the griminess of the job - but at the day's end I wanted to be clean. That put me in the minority. Most nights I was one out of 20 who made the trek to the shower trailers, when they were an option. There were men on my crew who did not see the point in showering every night if they were just going to get up the next day and get dirty all over again. Carlton, for example, made a point to not shower during fourteen-day rotations on fires. If cleanliness is next to Godliness then he was right alongside the devil himself.

In June of 2015, Carlton relayed to me following story. At the end of the previous fire season he had gone to the doctor because he was suffering hearing loss. However, he was more irate than thankful when the doctor restored his hearing. His anger came, not because the doctor had performed an emergency surgery, but because he had cured him with only a small amount of warm oil – by removing a large buildup of earwax and charging him $200 in the process. When I brought to his attention the correlation between his hearing loss/earwax stockpile with his affinity for not showering for two weeks at a time, he laughed if off as if I had told him the Earth was flat.

Chester was another proponent of not showering for days on end. I believe his unwillingness to shower was because he needed to confirm to himself that he was more than just a coastie (a derogatory term used by those east of the Cascade Mountains in Washington to denote both location and weakness of spirit). His choice was also an aesthetic one, as when he was on a fire he became a dirt magnet - ash and dirt clung to his face and filled in the patches where he lacked facial hair, effectively giving him a dirty beard i.e., the appearance of strength, the appearance of a man. Sadly, at the end of a fourteen day rotation, after he showered all traces of his dirt beard were gone, leaving the baby-faced coastie in its wake.

And if being dirty was likened to machismo, then during my second fire season, Patty was the Chuck Norris of us all. At the apex of the 2014 fire season, the Highlands 20 went on back-to-back-to-back fourteen-day rotations with only one R&R day off in between each rotation. This meant that for every fourteen days of fighting fire that we had 24-hours off to party (which took precedence over everything else), take care of life outside of fire (see girlfriends and wives, pay bills, go fishing, relax etc.) and do laundry – which, in retrospect, probably should have been the top priority.

It was during the second and third of those back-to-back-to-back rotations that on both R&R days Patty partied so hard that he neglected to wash the crusty socks and underwear in his red bag (an oversized duffel bag the Highlands 20 used to bring extra t-shirts, socks, and underwear when on fires). That coupled with his decision to not shower during each two-week roll (a total of 28 days) manifested in two disgusting ways.

1) He reeked. I don't mean that he smelled as if he had a bit of garlicky body odor. No Patty's stench was Biblical. When riding to and from the fires in our buggy the windows had to be down. His funk burnt our nostrils; it snapped against our tongues and brought tears to our eyes.

I recall being at the Okanogan County Fairgrounds where an ICP had been setup for the Carlton Complex. It was one of the rare times that we actually setup tents rather than just roll our sleeping bags out on the ground. As such, our 20 tents had been organized in two rows of ten between two livestock sheds. I was walking back from the shower trailer, enjoying not smelling of smoke, when, about 100 feet away, even before I had rounded the corner of the barn to our tent alley, I smelled Patty and his rotten-cheese-bloated-roadkill-morning-breath-chemical-warfare-stank. Which segues into the second disgusting manifestation.

2) As I entered our tent-lined passageway I saw not only the offensive smelling offender, I saw what he was doing and nearly lost my dinner. Patty was sitting in front of his tent, socks off, using a

pocketknife to scrape the fungus off of his feet; the product of his negligence – the price of manliness.

8.

Wildland firefighting can be an extremely demanding vocation with days on end spent on your feet, racing from fire-to-fire, as was the case in 2015 when Washington damn near burnt off the map. That year, shenanigans were at a low point. There was one day, however, that the temptation was so prime, so ripe that I couldn't resist.

It was mid-afternoon in the early days of June at the Highlands 20 Fire Camp; nestled in the primal Sinlahekin Valley. The sweet smell of pine warmed by the sun wafted through the air, the sky was cloudless, and the LAL (Lightning Activity Level – a good predictor of fires, the higher the level [1-6] the better the chances of a fire) was 1. My crew and I had spent the morning mowing grass, raking pine cones, moving toe-breaking-rocks from our volleyball court, and cleaning the already clean saw shop – anything we could to kill time and give the appearance of being busy – when we got the order to "gear up." Typically in situations like that it meant that we would be putting on our Yellows, helmets, and linepacks, grabbing our tools and going on a PT (Physical Training) hike until we were either off the clock or a fire broke. Our squadbosses had another plan for us.

We stood in STO beneath the punishing sun our unified acrid body odor overpowering any other scent on the scant breeze. We were then each handed a plastic grocery bag. I knew immediately what was to be done. We were going to practice 'gridding.' During the mop-up stage of a fire, meaning that the fire is essentially out, the burnt over areas are combed over to ensure that there are no smoldering bits that could reignite, 'gridding' is when wildland firefighters spread out in a line and walk the fire looking for smokes or hot spots. Our practice 'gridding,' however, was not to search for smokes or hot spots, but for trash.

Walter, a hefty man in his early thirties, and his rookie fire season, and who stood behind me in STO, asked me what the bags were for…and here is where I couldn't resist. I easily could have told him the truth, but instead told him that we were going to go for a hike with the plastic bags over our heads because the lack of air would simulate what it's like to be in a smoky environment. He did not question me or tell me

I was a liar. He immediately put his plastic bag over his head. I should have let him start ‘gridding,’ but after about 30-seconds of him standing in STO breathing heavily into the plastic bag, no doubt preparing himself for the hike he thought he was about to go on, the hike that Rio Hondo Fire Academy had never prepared him for, I had to confess that I was full of shit.

My rookie fire season (2013) was much different in terms of pranks. The fires were spread out and therefore the tomfoolery was far more prevalent, almost expected. On July 29, our third and final day on the Bear Creek Fire the Highlands 20 was mopping up our Division. I was a swamper on the saw team, which meant that we were only needed if there was something to cut, and since there was nothing to be cut it meant that I spent a large portion of that day sitting in the shade with my sawyer and our crewboss and listened to them swap stories of fires past, when Matt, our crewboss, got a call over the handheld radio. It was his boss, an older balding freckled ginger with a mustache that hung from his upper lip like a straw broom, who once said, “I wouldn’t want to be there when the gravy hits the road,” and who was especially touchy-feely with young female wildland firefighters always caressing their shoulders in a creepy-uncle-kind-of-way and making jokes that were not at all funny.

He had radioed Matt asking for the location of the archeological site that Matt had previously called in. Matt smiled his sly crooked-tooth-smile, and after getting his boss' coordinates told him that he was about two miles downhill from where he'd spotted it. His boss thanked him and commented that he had "one heck of a hike ahead of him." Matt snickered and told us that earlier that day, knowing that his boss was a prick and a shit hiker, he had found the steepest and nastiest part of the fire, way up on top of the ridge and had stacked some rocks in order to lure him up there to inspect the archeological site.

Since wildland firefighting involves intense physical labor it was common to knock out for a few minutes during lunch breaks. It was also common to wake up from those much needed naps to find that your linepack was a few pounds heavier. The culprit: rocks that had been stashed in the pouches.

Gonzalez was one of my favorite people on the Highlands 20. Raw.

Hilarious. Zero fucks given. He was an ex-Marine who brought a much different vibe to the crew. He had been in combat overseas and was very comfortable with his body. So comfortable that he would flash his penis randomly just to get a laugh. You never knew when he would strike. You could be digging fireline or standing in STO or sitting in the buggy or even at a crowded redneck bar in Omak, Washington. Wherever the setting, the scenario was always the same: Gonzalez would call your name, you would turn to see what he wanted, he would then stare at you without saying a word - his eyebrows pushing together behind black rim glasses, you'd then glance down and see flesh where a zipper should be. I'm not sure if he was putting his hook out there waiting for a bite or if he just knew how to make everyone uncomfortable, but whatever the case it never failed to get a few chuckles and lighten even the darkest of moods.

Pranks acted as rituals; performed to garner laughs, relieve stressful situations, and despite their maliciousness were never meant to cause serious harm – discomfort, yes – but never harm. They were also learning exercises, because after each prank we discovered a little more about each other, slowly evolving, finding our place in our tribe, learning exactly what it meant to be a crewmember of the Highlands 20...and then there was Nelson.

On my rookie fire season Nelson was the least likely guy to be on the fire crew. He was the one that everybody put odds on when he would quit. There's always one. Fleshy. Pasty. Computer-nerdy. Carried a ninja throwing star in his wallet, constantly pushed his glasses up the bridge of his nose, and was detested for being a nonstop smartass, and especially for his reply of, "Gee, life's tough," spoken in a sarcastic monotone, in response to Judy (our elderly Fire Camp cook) after telling him she had had breast cancer. Needless to say he was the butt of two pranks, not very imaginative ones, but effective just the same.

The first week of each of the fire seasons that I've worked were filled with long and dry meetings; meetings that were informative but nonetheless boring and took every ounce of willpower you could muster not to fall asleep in. The meetings either consisted of training sessions for rookies or refresher classes for seasoned wildland firefighters. The information presented was useful but presented in such a dull governmental way that you'd spend most of the time lost in thought, pondering how your life choices culminated in you sitting right then and there.

During those sessions the presenter would randomly ask questions to the audience – to make sure that the audience was both conscious and aware that the information could someday save their life. It was during those sessions, the first week of my rookie fire season that Nelson would be called on, and each time he proceeded to give the most smart-aleck answers he could. Yes, his answers did get a laugh from all in the room, but his wise guy answers reflected bad on us, his fire crew, the Highlands 20.

At the week's end, everyone had been cooped up in Fire Camp learning about their summer vocation and needed to spread their wings and fluff their tail feathers. What that entailed was having Mexican food and tequila shots in Tonasket before heading south to Walmart for groceries. I rode with the Cali Boys (Gonzalez, Rich, and Andy), and, as you do on rural American roads, we drank cheap canned beer along the way. On the trip back to Fire Camp – somewhere between Riverside and Loomis – the subject of Nelson and his wiseass comments came up, to the dismay of all of our vehicles occupants. When we reached our home for the summer we strolled into the barracks half-drunk and realized no one else had made it back from town yet. Now I'm not going to try and defend our next actions or make excuses, this is just the straight fact of what we did. Seeing that the barracks were sans crew, we got the bright idea that the best way to get back at Nelson was the childish-passive-aggressive-move of wiping our balls and bare-asses with his pillow. As I type these words, I'm shaking my head and laughing, though I am a believer in karma and fear that one day, I, too, will sleep on an assy-ballsy-pillow, if I haven't already. The best part was waking up on Saturday morning to see Nelson curled up in the fetal position in his bunk, his face buried in the pillow that, hours before had wiped our genitalia clean.

Males are dirty by nature. This is fact. Especially when there are no females to keep them in check or make them abide by the rules of decent society. Showers become less frequent. Beer takes the place of water. You say less 'thank you's' and more 'fuck you's.' You tend to revert to apish cavemen who form their own cliques – usually divided into two categories: the strong and the weak. At Fire Camp it was no different, sort of like *Lord of the Flies* only without all the murder.

Nelson fell into the category of the weak. One hot August night in 2013, after having endured almost a full fire season of his smartass remarks and lack of caring about how his actions reflected on the rest of the fire crew, a group of us had had enough (both of alcohol and Nelson's bullshit). How did we deal with the situation? In the most immature and primate way possible. With a full moon overhead and a choir of crickets to score our actions – we urinated all over his Jeep Cherokee: from the door handles, to the windshield, to the grill. If memory serves someone even pissed into his gas tank. Luckily, he had locked his vehicle otherwise I have no doubt we would have doused the cloth seats as well. But despite all the shit that he more than earned from the crew, at the end of the day he was still one of us.

9.

It was nighttime on August 19, 2013, sometime between ten and eleven that night. The Highlands 20 had been fighting a breakneck uphill battle with the forest fire that was consuming the mountains outside of Leavenworth, Washington. We had arrived at 5pm, geared up, hiked in, and spent the next five hours performing a direct attack – cutting fireline as close to the fire as possible. I was a sawyer on that fire and led the charge up the mountain, using my chainsaw to cleave the burning trees, forming a path for the diggers on the crew to follow, choking down lungful's of smoke, tears ran from my eyes, my nostrils became faucets for snot, and every few feet I would be so overwhelmed by the chokingly thick smoke that I'd drop to my knees and suck in as much clean air as possible before rising up to continue my assault.

After five hours of struggling and cutting and eating smoke, we, the saw team, (Cody, Jeff, Taylor, and myself) had reached the mountain's peak and had tied into the black. This meant that we had connected our fireline with the area of the forest that had already burnt over. There, we waited for the diggers to complete the fireline through the denuded swath we had created.

Gonzalez once told me a valuable proverb, "Why run when you can walk, why stand when you can sit, why sit when you can lie down." And at that moment, we were lying down, our backs propped up against our linepacks, giving our bodies a rest we had more than earned. Around us the night was black, all except for the inviting soft orange glow from the trees that still burned and smoldered. In those thin knives of light we sat and ate. That was another rule of wildland firefighting – eat when you can because you might not get the chance for a long while.

With our feet splayed out in front of us we dug into our MREs (Meals Ready to Eat – the dehydrated food of soldiers that was a must that we carry in our linepacks). As we slogged our way through tuna with noodles, and cheese and vegetable omelets - meals whose flavors were closer to a sweaty cardboard box than what was stated on the package - the four of us began to fantasize out loud.

These fantasies were far from sexual. They were culinary. We talked about our dream meals, what we would eat if we could have anything at that moment. I had Panang curry with chicken fried rice in mind, and not the watery mess they call curry in Thai restaurants in the States, but the thick gravy-like-curry I had eaten on the streets in Thailand. Jeff spoke of his craving for sushi and sake, a simple and clean meal without much fuss – light on the stomach with an airy buzz. Cody's meal was more traditional and I envisioned served on fine china by a waiter wearing a tuxedo with tails and a haughty look on his face – prime rib with au jus and horseradish, a twice-baked potato, a hand tossed Caesar salad, and a bottle of pinot noir. Taylor's meal was more of a feast than a meal. He wanted roast beef with gravy, turkey and stuffing, a pepperoni pizza, fried chicken, a cheeseburger, a plate of spaghetti and meatballs, barbecued ribs, and coleslaw, and Jell-O with whip cream, a whole strawberry cheesecake and a chocolate milkshake to wash it all down. We laughed at his stomach-blowout, but it didn't surprise us as, though he was fit, he had earned the nickname of the 'fat kid,' due to his insatiable junk food habit.

The succulent delusions that hung above our heads in thought bubbles reminded us of who we were, that we were more than just bodies to throw at a forest fire. We were dreamers and doers, sons and brothers, students and lovers. By breaking parched (and tasteless) bread together, after earning every inch of our way to that mountaintop reprieve, as the rest of the crew caught up to us, I understood, maybe a little more than the rest of them, that what we were sharing was meaningful; for it is not in the good times and pleasurable meals that people truly reveal themselves, but in times of lack and distress. Wildland firefighting might have been the bricks of our fraternal order but it was hardship that was the mortar that held us together.

10.

At the end of every fire season there was an adjustment period. You were so used to the company of the crew, their own unfiltered way of being, that when all the fires had been defeated and it was time to return from whence you came; it always took a few weeks to once again adjust to the confines of society. No longer could you burp and fart in the company of others without being perceived as crude. Long gone were the days of hiking and cutting fireline and living in filth. Modes of speech had to be modified. People looked at you sideways when you said things like, "I'm just gonna bump around you," or "Moving," when you filed through the checkout line at the supermarket. Your ratio of curse words to non-dirty words also had to be adjusted accordingly. I remember physically having to stop myself mid-sentence when talking to my mother post-fire season, my brain scrambling for words that she would not take offense to, yet that would still convey the emotional punch of the story I was telling.

The adjustment period included a reintroduction to life. Sleeping in. Eating food that wasn't chalked full of fart inducing preservatives. Showering alone. Wearing whatever you want, whenever you wanted to. Drinking as much coffee as you could without the fear of inducing dehydration. Getting high in the morning. Getting drunk at night. Wearing flip-flops, and not just in the shower. Being around women. All the things that had been denied during fire season became new again. It felt as if you had been reborn a full-grown virgin into the world.

My rookie fire season I left Fire Camp on September 15. September 16 found me on Venice Beach, California. There was sunshine, music, the lull of waves in the distance; people of every variety walked the boardwalk in droves, the smell of smoke was in the air – incense and marijuana smoke, that is. A four-story mural of Jim Morrison kept a watchful eye over me as colorful hawkers and artists sold their wares. The vibe was light and positive. A music video was being shot with a cadre of bubblegum chewing, bikini clad women on roller skates. It was the antithesis of the Highlands 20 Fire Camp. I was in Heaven.

I texted pictures back to my crew who were still in the wilds of Washington, knowing that it would be hours until they were again in cell service. I wanted to show them all that I saw – not to make them jealous, well, maybe just a little jealous, but mostly, to let them know that the 'real' world still existed, that just beyond the end of their fire season lay paradise.

It never failed, though. Months would pass and you would be in the 'real' world – in class taking notes on Beowulf, or at a brewery enjoying a beer - when you would see someone wearing a fire crew shirt or hear a string of random words that would trigger your inner wildland firefighter. The next thing you knew you would be jonesing to be back at Fire Camp, back in the woods where life was simpler, where there was a distinct goal, far from conveniences and people who never would or could understand you, back to where the only thing that mattered was fighting wildfire and laughing with your fire crew. Though the times had been tough when you were out there, and you had vowed never to go do it again because it was too hard on your body, too hard on your relationships, too hard on your psyche, it had still left an indelible mark on your soul and you would never be the same again.

11.

What if my time on the Highlands 20 had been some grand social experiment? One in which 20 men from 20 different backgrounds, were removed from the familiar, from those they knew and loved, and set loose upon each other in a harsh and challenging environment. The result would find that rather than dispersing like ash in the wind, we instead became one, we became a tribe, we became fire brothers.

If we hadn't, our lives would have been harder than they already were. It wasn't easy doing what we did, what was expected of us, and coming together as one was our only way to survive. We sweated together. We earned blisters together. We ate smoke together. We took meals together. We had each other's backs and gave advice - whether it was asked for or not. We laughed at each other. We comforted each other. We listened to each other. Our lives became intertwined in a way that can never be undone.

Fire Camp is just a series of memories for me, some bad, but most good, and like all my memories: the bad fade to the dark recesses of the mind while I keep the good close to my heart. Sometimes I run across mementos from those seasons in my life – a faded Highlands 20 crew t-shirt stained with bar oil and the flashbacks that will never lose color, a copy of an *IRPG* (*Incident Response Pocket Guide*) rests on my bookshelf – and each time I see it, a feeling of gratitude wells up inside of me.

Through the years that have passed, since I last donned a Yellow and a linepack, my tribe has grown smaller, only keeping track of a few of those who were significant during those years. Chester went on to father a fire baby (a child conceived during a fire season) and that this year (2018) he says will be his last season as a wildland firefighter, a Hotshot crewmember, to be exact. Patty is a Hotshot as well. Taylor left the world of wildland firefighting and is living in North Central Washington doing his best to navigate his way through life. Gonzalez (one-third of the Cali Boys) is a structure firefighter for Los Angeles County and has confessed to making an obscene amount of money doing so. Matt was involved in a serious car accident and is still recovering. Rich and Andy (the other two-thirds of the Cali Boys) are on a wildland firefighting crew in Ventura County. I often think about Fire Camp, about the Highlands 20, and how it changed me. Writing about it helps me clarify its lingering significance, but I have yet to scratch the surface of its true implications.

2018

The Curious Case of the Dryer Shitter

The Highlands 20 Fire Crew 2013, minus myself and the squadbosses and crewboss.

Left to right (standing): Eric, Jeff, Cody, Nelson, Gonzalez, Sam, Chester, Valle, and Patty.
Left to right (kneeling): Derek, Rich, Andy, and Taylor.

I want to tell you where I was the day of August 9th, 2013, and why I was sitting in the cool cement-floored barracks of the Highlands 20 Fire Camp listening to Frank, my saw team leader, brief us about that upcoming night, because the entire time I was unaware that a mystery was about to unfold that still haunts me to this day.

The Highlands 20 Fire Camp sits in the Ponderosa Pine and Douglas Fir rich Sinlahekin Valley of North Central Washington, an isolated area cut off from civilization that the Cali Boys called "the boonies."

Some twenty-five miles South of the Canadian border, the landscape, with its sheer rock sidewalls rising from the valley floor and its proximity to a town of any size (Omak, Washington population: 4776 and 36 miles away), makes it an ideal location for a fire camp. The locals speak of horses and cattle and orchard crops, and wear Wranglers and cowboy boots and pearl snap shirts, not as a fashion statement, but as a way of life. The land is steep and unforgiving, and views are the very definition of majestic; rattlesnakes, groups of white tail deer, numerous pristine lakes that dot the area and act as an oasis to locals and those in the know. It is a place where both cellphone and Internet service are only dreams and nothing more.

The Highlands 20 Fire Camp itself is a congregation of eight buildings separated by a gravel road, a community unto its own, bounded on the North by the defunct A-frame chapel turned weight room, and to the East – the saw shop and various outbuildings, followed by the office, the mess hall. On the South end of camp the barracks, which resemble the shape of a pipe cut in half; its rounded roof of corrugated sheet-metal and its solid concrete floors a constant cool temperature even on days that peak 100 degrees, which are frequent. It is there that I sat and listened to Frank.

I relay this to you because you need to understand precisely what can happen when you separate men from civilization for months at a time and leave them to their own devices in the middle of nowhere.

The Highlands 20 saw team leader, Frank, was twenty-six years old, and had been a wildland firefighter for eight seasons at that point, having spent the majority of his time on the Highlands 20. He had also been on a hotshot crew for a season or two. He was a strawberry blonde who stood over six feet tall, gangly yet strong, and quick to correct your chainsaw cuts with a flick on your knuckles with a thin metal rod, and he was always, always ready for a cold beer.

We had just finished fourteen days on the Clockum Tarps Fire earning us a single yet hallowed day off, an R&R day, and it just so happened that our twenty-four hours free from fire landed on the Friday night of the Omak Stampede & World Famous Suicide Race.

At 4:30pm we were off the clock. By a quarter to five we were all showered and shaved, readying ourselves for a rough and tumble night on the town. While we were in the barracks dousing cologne and putting on our 'going to town clothes,' Frank had us all gather around so he could give us a briefing. You see, first thing every morning during fire seasons, a briefing was held. These briefings were meant to inform us of that day's goings on – everything from predicted weather and wind conditions, to available resources, to the details of our mission. Frank's briefing, however, was not a fire briefing, but a party briefing.

Situation: Omak, Washington – host of the Omak Stampede and World Famous Suicide Race, an annual rodeo and powwow that was estimated to increase the town's population to 20,000 over the course of the five day event. What this meant to us was that there would be a hell of a lot of eligible cowgirls in tight fitting jeans.

Mission: to eat, drink, smoke, dance, and get laid – basically anything we could do to forget about fighting wildfire for 24 hours and remind ourselves that we were more than just expendable pieces in that summer's ongoing fight with Nature.

Communication: the comm. plan was simple – stick together. If we had to leave the crew the buddy system was to be employed. If all else failed we had cell service within Omak city limits, though, with the expected level of drunken shenanigans cellphones were a last resort.

Risk Management: we were warned to be careful of whom we danced or went home with as in the past jealous cowboys and shitfaced natives had been known to start scraps with anyone they saw as a threat to their claim on the local females, i.e., our testosterone heavy crew. Because if one of us got in a fight, that meant we all got into a fight.

The night in question had been a roaring success, minus the getting laid part, as none of the females we encountered were as erotically charged (or as desperate) as we were. We did manage to blot out all thoughts of fire and with the help of a delicious meal, large amounts of alcohol, and dancing with cowgirls, we once again felt human. We all ended our night partying till we had passed out at Frank's sister's place in town, all except Warner (who had opted not to leave Fire Camp because of his antisocial tendencies), Matt (who had spent the night with his family) and six others (Larsen, Jeff, Cody, Nelson, Valle, and Eric) who made the hour long drive back to Fire Camp rather than play beer pong till the sun swapped places with the moon.

10 August 2013 began as an ordinary hungover day, one of those days when your guts feel like they're trying to eat their way out of your asshole, and you have trouble jumpstarting your thoughts due to the homemade moonshine still sloshing around in your skull.

Let me set the scene. I wake up on a couch, the sun piercing through the window, heating me past the point of comfort, cooking me in my own juices. I immediately felt sorry for all ants that fall prey to sadistic boys with magnifying glasses. As I leaned up on my elbows to survey the spectacle that had been the previous nights drunkfest, I was first greeted with a minefield of half-eaten corn chips spread across my chest and stomach, and around me, on the floor, were the rest of my crew - the ones who had stayed that is – sprawled in all manner of disarray and cramp-inducing positions throughout the living room, kitchen, and, viewed from the window I could see Chester passed out on the front lawn. Face up. Mouth open. Tongue out, as if he were dreaming of catching snowflakes. One by one the rest of my crew began to wake, each of them letting out slow, low moans usually reserved for zombies in B-horror movies, followed by the exact same question: what the hell happened last night? The Highlands 20, or, rather the Highlands 12 happened last night, I thought.

With everyone up and about, we collected ourselves, and all the crushed beer cans strewn about the front yard like deformed metallic daisies, and piled into our respective vehicles to begin our drive to the tranquility of the Highlands 20 Fire Camp; more than ready to sleep off the remnants of our R&R.

We followed US 97 North out of Omak along the Okanogan River, flanked on both sides by mountains, where sagebrush as far as the eye could see clung brown and dead on the stalk, making the cloudless blue sky appear richer and more velvety in texture. At the one-stoplight town of Tonasket, its main drag lined with stores and shops that had yet to be touched by the fingers of corporate America, where people waved to one another as they passed in their pickup trucks, and we turned onto Highway 7.

From there, the complexion of the landscape changed from high desert browns, tans, and beiges to the lush verdant greens of orchard country. Still forming apples sagged heavy on branches. The same sun that had burnt me awake formed rainbows in the arcs of water spat out by the countless rows of sprinklers.

With the windows down it smelled of new life, of hope.

We exited Highway 7 and headed west on the Loomis-Oroville Road, freshwater lakes and fields of alfalfa soon replaced the orchards. Farmers bailed hay. Cows gnawed grass. And from Loomis, a village with a population of 159, we headed south on Sinlahekin Road for the three miles back to our home for the summer: Highlands 20 Fire Camp.

Warner, our squadboss, greeted us in the parking area. As We, the Cali Boys and I, poured ourselves from the black Honda, the first of those who'd stayed the night at Frank's sisters to arrive at Fire Camp,

Stroking the bush of hair that grew only from his chin, his eyes bloodshot, Warner cleared his throat, and said, "Alright, well I know it wasn't you guys because you just rolled into camp."

The Cali Boys and I looked from one to another, confused.

"What's up?" I asked.

Warner ran a finger between his lower lip and gum and slung a wad of chewing tobacco onto the gravel before answering, "Someone shit the dryer last night," his delivery humorless.

The four of us snickered; ribbing each other at the ludicrous prank that Warner was obviously playing on us.

He snapped his fingers to quell our laughter. He went on to tell us he was serious and that whoever it was hadn't just shit the dryer; they had shit the dryer full of Larsen's clothes and had turned it on ruining both the dryer and every piece of clothing Larsen had brought to Fire Camp.

His deadpan inflection only added fuel to our snickering, which snowballed into full-on-gut-busting-laughter.

Warner, too, began to laugh right along with us before stopping suddenly. Both his face and voice void of mirth, he vowed that he would find whoever was responsible as if he were going to investigate the murder of a relative, vigilante style.

That was 11am.

Fourteen hours later his investigation really began when he burst into the squad one barracks, hit the lights and yelled these four words, "Wake up you motherfuckers!"

Unlike me, who had spent my R&R day recovering from the previous nights bout with booze, Warner had spent his drinking, and from the sounds of it, heavily. What followed was a twenty-minute raging-whiskey-fueled-meltdown, the highlights of which included:

- Going nose-to-nose with every stunned member of Squad One, questioning his intentions to fight fire
- Telling us (Squad One) that we would never be Type One Firefighters
- Making outrageous (and untrue) claims about our testicles
- Insisting that we "did not know crazy" and that he'd "seen blood."
- Challenging all of Squad One to a seven-on-one brawl

At the end of his tirade, he had sobered up enough to realize that we were not the enemy but his subordinates, he exited our barracks the way he entered: loud, profane, and angry. He shouted, "And I want to know...who shit the g**damn dryer?!"

At that point, we all wanted to know who shit the dryer.

19 August 2013 was a bright warm day in Okanogan County, the kind of day where bald eagles float on the breeze, and the sharp, sweet, refreshing smell of pine lingers in the air. We, the Highlands 20, were once again back home at the Highlands 20 Fire Camp after spending seven days on the Silver Star Fire. It was 9:15am on a Monday morning. Briefing had just ended and since we had not yet been called to another fire, Warner had all of us – minus Matt - come down to the laundry room to witness a forensic test.

During the course of the previous week, during the Silver Star Fire, Warner had done his best Magnum PI impersonation and deduced that there were only six people in camp who could have "shit the dryer" – Eric, Cody, Nelson, Jeff, Valle, and Larsen, however, Larsen was not a suspect as the likelihood of him shitting on his own clothes was far-fetched. With all of us, the fire crew, in attendance, Warner took the five suspects and had them one at a time bend over and put their butts into the remaining front-loading dryer, because “the shit dryer,” as it had come to be known, had been moved to a shed to avoid drawing unnecessary heat from other wildland firefighting officials who shared our laundry facilities, and who would definitely not find the humor in one of their own shitting the dryer.

Nelson, a thick-glasses wearing young man, whose tendency to make constant uncalled-for remarks often resulted in countless punishing P.T. hikes for his squad, Squad Two, was the first suspect. He tottered and teetered and tried to balance on the balls of his feet, but alas he was unable to balance long enough to fit himself into the dryer. Verdict: not guilty.

Eric, soft spoken with the face of a bear cub and an insane love for the Seattle Seahawks, was the tallest of the five suspects. He squatted down and fit his ass into the mouth of the dryer with ease. Verdict: possibly guilty.

Valle, who had wiry ginger hair and was going to school to be a dentist, and who would wear both his gloves and helmet when riding in the buggy to and from fires (because, safety first), was the third suspect.

He, like Nelson, wiggled and wobbled yet could not find the balance to plug himself into the dryer. Verdict: not guilty.

Jeff – the most "granola" man on the crew – recent graduate of Western Washington University and aficionado of roll-your-own-cigarettes and owner of a Tom Selleck mustache. He was the fourth suspect. He hunched over and backed himself slowly but surely into the dryer's gape. He also confessed that though he did not think he had shat the dryer, he was unsure, as he had blacked out the Friday night in question. Verdict: not guilty. I say not guilty only because the squadbosses deemed it so. Also, Jeff was far too polite to ever shit the dryer, even in a blacked out state.

Cody, the crew's resident eccentric. Loathed by the overhead yet liked by me. He was known for his rainbow suspenders and his penchant for doing gymnastics moves and yoga poses on the fireline. He once told me that he would not be returning for another fire season as it coincided with circus season, and he'd always dreamed of being a clown. He was the final suspect to place his derriere in the dryer and he did so with the delicate ease of a contortionist bending in half. Verdict: possibly guilty.

Warner followed his ass-in-the-dryer forensic test by individually questioning each of us, the crew, who we thought had perpetrated the fecal transgression. He was left with two possible dryer shitters: Cody and Eric. Jeff was no longer a suspect due to it being entirely out of character for him. As for Valle and Nelson, well, if the ass didn't fit, he must acquit.

As for Cody and Eric, both were at Fire Camp the night in question, both were admittedly very drunk – therefore their alibis were ruled worthless, and both of them had had verbal altercations with Larsen throughout that fire season. And, of course, when each of them was asked point blank by Warner if they had done it, they had denied the accusations. Seriously though, despite the fact that it was a complete laugh riot, who in their right mind would confess to an irritable ex-Marine (Warner) that they had shit the dryer? Also, I can only speculate that if either had confessed it would have resulted in their immediate termination and the purchase of a new dryer for Fire Camp.

07 September 2013 the plot thickened...After a few more weeks of

hopping from fire-to-fire, our fire season began to wind down and with it we had a proper two-day weekend off. A few of us, including myself, had gone back to our numerous hometowns across Washington, while the rest of the crew, including Cody and Nelson, made their way to Ellensburg to party their two days away at Chester's house.

It was at said party that another shit related incident occurred. Despite my not being there, here is how the episode was relayed to me. Chester had hosted a party at his house, something akin to a party from *Animal House* or *Old School*, as he lived in a raucous college town and was known for throwing raucous college town house parties. In attendance: two of the dryer shitter suspects – Cody and Nelson. During the night a partygoer went to the front porch for a cigarette and nearly stepped on a pile of fresh human logs plopped onto the welcome mat. Again, both of them were questioned, though this time by Chester and Warner, but the result was the same: both fiercely denied the charge. However, it fared worse for Cody's case than Nelson's since everyone suspected that Cody was the original dryer shitter.

15 September 2013 was the final day of fire season for me as I had a

plane to catch to Los Angeles the next day, a week of fun in the sun before I was to crawl back into my books and hunker down for another year at college. My final day consisted of checking in the gear I had been issued by the State – linepack, sleeping bag, first aid kit, etc. At the end of the day, just before I was to exit Fire Camp, Matt and Warner, my crewboss and squadboss, conducted a final evaluation.

The final evaluation consisted of them reviewing my performance over the course of the fire season and asking me two final questions, where the answer of the first led to the answer of the second. Had I find out who the dryer shitter was? Would I return for another fire season? I answered both questions honestly. I had no idea who had shit the dryer, and, if I had to base all my previous summers on laughter alone, that summer of 2013 had been the best summer of my entire life, and I would definitely be back for the sequel the following year.

30 January 2018. As I type these words and think about where I am and the man that I have become, I am still troubled by the fact that I do not know who shit the dryer five years ago. Though my squadbosses had

pegged Cody as the dryer shitter, my suspicions were that it was Eric, mainly because I did not like Eric and due to the perfect ease with which he corked his bum into the dryer during the forensic test. I refused to believe it was Cody because he was my friend and second favorite swamper (I was my first favorite). Yet, I have asked Cody throughout the years if he had done it, and each time he has denied the crime, and I am compelled to believe him. The curious case of the dryer shitter, for me, ranks up there with the great mysteries of life that I will never know the answer to, such as who built the pyramids and if 9/11 was an inside job.

2018

My Midlife Rite of Passage

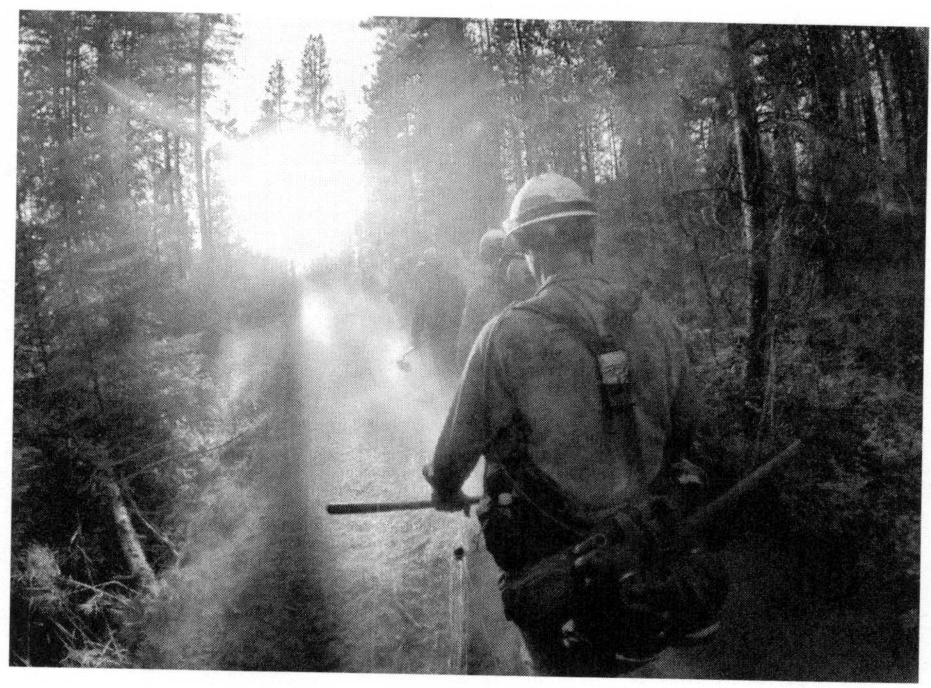

A Picture of my back as the Highlands 20 and I hike out of the Silver Creek Fire (2014). Photo Credit: Jimmy Gonzalez

Because I owed my father eight hundred dollars and had no love in my life and had lived as the prodigal son – traveling the world, debauching away all of my 401k, returning home with zero dollars in my bank account - and having survived a battle with Dengue Fever, and was in my mid-thirties and in my first year of college, and therefore every penny earned was spent to fund my education, I took a job as a wildland firefighter, a line of work that demands much of your body and more of your soul and where the median age is twenty-one.

In that line of work I could find what I sought, alongside small town boys with high school educations and ambitions that didn't reach beyond their city limit signs, there with those who wanted to fight fire as a career and the graduates of the Rio Hondo Fire Academy and the aimless lads in need of direction and the wanderers and the renegades and the misfits and those who wanted to live the life of mountain men. We were all there because we could make a fat wad of cash in a short amount of time: as I was told, an estimated $15,000 in three months, but as I found out over the course of my four fire seasons it was more than just money that I sought. Unbeknownst to me, there was a beast within. It howled from its confines brought on by stagnant and sedentary living, it bit and scratched at the bars of its invisible prison; and it wasn't until I became a wildland firefighter that I was to find the key to its cage.

Though I had already accomplished much in my evolution as a man before joining: losing my virginity, moving out of my parents' home, starting a career, living abroad – I had reached a stalemate in life: no longer was I a young man, yet I was years away from the middle age as resembled by many others around me, being tied down with mortgages and kids. I was in the midst of my thirties and had come to a split in the road. One path would kill me softly as I dwindled what was left of my youth holding down a job that made “good money,” and settling down to give my parents grandchildren. The other path was one that held less security, less safety, yet also, less monotony, less boredom, thus less of an opportunity to feel like I had hung myself in pursuit of the supposed American dream.

Never having wanted to live a dull life, I chose the latter of the two paths, the one which to me represented freedom and adventure. Through this I was to shed the societal binds I had grown accustomed to. I was to live dirty and do backbreaking work and forget that I was a decade or more closer to the grave than those around me. I was to find strength, both inner and outer, that I had always known were in me but had somehow forgotten along the way, letting that muscle of spirit atrophy. I was to find out for myself that just beyond what I thought were my limits were not despair but where true growth began.

I went into wildland firefighting with no preconceptions of what to expect. No one had told me stories about the job. I had never read a book or watched a film about the subject. Even those who I knew who were wildland firefighters had never spoken a word about it other than that was what they did during the summer. And maybe it was for the best. Because had I known what all would have been asked of me, required of me, expected of me, I cannot honestly say if I would have done it. I have no desire to woo you with fire-filled tales of bravery or claim to be the biggest badass who ever wore Nomex and wielded a chainsaw. Now that you know that I lack all inclination to indulge in acts of self-heroism, honest or exaggerated, I am going to do my best to explain how and why wildland firefighting changed me, broke the shell of who I was, never to be the same again, and forged me into the man that I am today. The memories of life lived as a wildland firefighter will remain with me until my last breath, long after the smell of timber smoke and the growl of chainsaws and the heat of the flames on my naked face fade to nothingness.

I often laugh when I think about who I am as a human and the odd and strange things from my past that molded me into my present self. For example: my philosophy on life. It can be traced back to my childhood, not from anything my parents said, or stories from the Bible, or Saturday morning cartoons, no, it came from the most unlikely of sources: Emilio Estevez - from the 1988 film, *Young Guns*, a western that portrays the life and times of Billy the Kid. In one scene, Emilio, as Billy, says, "You've got to test yourself everyday, gentlemen. Once you stop testing yourself you get slow. When that happens, they kill you." Though Billy was talking to his compadres, challenging them to face their fears and to fight, my spongy ten-year-old brain soaked up those words, twisting them into this paraphrase: you've got to test yourself everyday to make sure that you're alive.

Testing myself, knowing my limits and going just a bit farther in order to become more today than I was the day before. That is exactly how I have tried to live my life. The key word in that previous sentence: "tried."

Looking back, there are plenty of times that I took the easy way out, but there are also just as many times that I did indeed live by the grit of Billy's rally cry. Working as an Alaskan fisherman, planting trees in the wilds of Oregon and Idaho, moving to Los Angeles with nothing but the clothes on my back and the determination not to fail, gaining employment in a production company, then giving up that very same employment and financial security for years of travel and personal growth, working my way through university and coming out debt free, to then teach English abroad. These are a list of challenges that I have placed before myself and feel pride for accomplishing. Yet the greatest test, the greatest opportunity for growth, came through wildland firefighting.

I went into my rookie fire season a man - by reckoning of age alone – yet still very much a boy at heart. I laughed at dick and fart jokes (still do), masturbated every chance that arose (still do) and had a problem with authority (still do). From the outside looking in, I was 34, the age that most would consider one to be a mature adult, the age where one has their life together, or is supposed to. Where I grew up in the Pacific Northwest men at that age had families and mortgages; wives and kids to feed, two-week annual vacations and barbecues with in-laws and whose greatest joy in life stemmed from fantasy football. Yet I was an outlier. I was an adult on paper, but in truth, I was just as lost as I had been at eighteen maybe even a little more so because I no longer had the shield of youth to hide behind.

I was in my thirties and in the midst of restarting my life. Once again I found myself in the same predicament I had been in in high school – broke, living with my parents, no prospects of romantic love and my self-esteem was the equivalent of a steaming dog turd on a winters morn. It would be a lie to say that I wasn't in the throes of depression, or at least standing upon the precipice of that black abyss.

However, what I did have going for me was a plan. After traveling for two years through Asia, I returned to my parents' home in the spring of 2012 to recover from breakbone fever (a far sexier and more accurate name for Dengue Fever), and for the first time in a long time I found myself rudderless; my life had no set course, no direction. With nothing but time on my hands I mulled the subject over and came to the following conclusions: I wanted to live abroad again, and not just for a few years but for the rest of my life; to do that I wanted to teach English, to do that I had to go to college. Though financial aid was generous and paid for most of my education, I was otherwise strapped.

So, come spring of 2013, I desired to be financially independent, to do that: I needed a job, still wanting to go to college fulltime and not work on top of my school load, I needed a summer job – one that paid a hell of a lot. In my small Washington town there were two legal options for men like me: working in the rough and tumble oil fields of North Dakota or battling Nature by fighting forest fires.

After contacting friends in both industries, the opportunity to become a wildland firefighter presented itself, and I jumped at the chance. Being a believer in the 'fake it till you make it,' philosophy, I did just that. I battened down the hatches on my shortcomings and depression, and went into the interview channeling my inner John Wayne - projecting as much steely perseverance as I could muster. Which must have been just enough, because, a few days later, the call came. The job was mine.

One month later I became a full-fledged member of the Highlands 20. There, I could not fake fortitude. I had to own it. There was just too much on the line (life, health, let's not forget pride – and not just mine, but that of my crew) not to have fortitude. After coming out of nine months of college, a place that leans towards desmasculinization through intellectualization, I was thrust into an adrenaline-fueled-alpha-male-physical-over-mental-environment...and it was just what I needed.

I had never played sports in high school or been in the military or a fraternity. Hell, I was never even in the Boy Scouts. The Highlands 20 was the first time that I had been exposed to a society made up exclusively of males. For me, being on the crew, chopping it up with men far younger than myself - always trying to out do each other, out tough each other, out drink each other; always talking about getting laid and laughing at crass jokes and generally acting like hellions – it was the shot of pure testosterone that I needed to wake me from the motionless mid-life slumber that unfortunately seems normal for men my age to succumb to.

I slipped into that state of mind, that way of being, as easy as putting on a pair of cowboy boots (which, if you never have, is extremely easy – there's no laces). Being in my mid-thirties and feeling the wane in my worth as a man in the "real" world, I found myself, and my place, amongst the Highlands 20. I was part of a brotherhood in the truest sense of the word. My role on the crew was that of the wise sage/world traveler/libertine, sort of a dirty old man version of Obi-Wan Kenobi. I was the one that the others looked to for advice: on life, on love (on second thought, I might not have been the best qualified to give advice on either subject). I was the one who always had a story at the ready of things that I had seen or done on foreign sands. I was the one who planned and executed bawdy escapades at the seasons end, and made sure to tell my crewmates every seedy detail the following year. As a wildland firefighter I found what Ponce de Leon had searched long and hard for; amongst my fire brothers, amongst the long days and the short nights, amongst the flames and the smoke and the soot and the goal of ending each fire season with my coffers filled with gold and the glory of every uphill battle we had fought with Nature - I discovered my very own Fountain of Youth.

Perhaps it seems not surprising that one of the main pillars of wildland firefighting is physical strength. If it does come as a shock...well, I'm sorry to burst your bubble. The reality of the situation is this: it is not a job for the weak (mentally, emotionally, but especially, physically). I am not talking about all wildland firefighting - as working on a fire engine or a rotor (helicopter) tends to make one soft. I am referring to the handcrews, the hotshots, the smokejumpers; those who are on their feet for sixteen hour shifts for weeks on end, and who hike into places that are inaccessible to vehicles, all while humping in chainsaws and tools and gallons of water and food and fire shelters and fuel and bar oil and extra chains and handheld radios and first aid kits and weather kits and all manner of odds and ends in their linepacks. For those reasons physical fitness is a must.

As the eldest wildland firefighter on the Highlands 20 for three consecutive fire seasons (not counting my squadboss or crewboss – one year and eight years my senior, respectively - who supervised the grunt work while I partook in it) I understood the importance of staying fit. I was not a young buck that could eat junk and not workout and always be fire ready. No, I had to work hard to keep up with my fire crew, harder than the rest, as my fleeting youth acted as a Gale-force wind that pushed hard against me. My body would no longer snap back into place like a rubber band after nights on end of moonlit beer benders. That is not to say that I was a strong hiker, like most of my other crewmembers were, (fact is: I was a shit hiker but what I lacked in speed, I made up for in stamina – or, at least that's what I told myself) or even the strongest member of the crew, but I held my own.

To do this I had to brutalize myself. I had to act as if weakness was a demon, and I was an exorcist, intent on casting it from my body. At Fire Camp, I kept a strict PT (Physical Training) schedule. Everyday after hours I would either run hills or strength train. And every time that I felt that my hips were about to pop out of their sockets, or my lungs burnt nuclear hot or my back was as stiff as dried cement I would remind myself that the pain I was feeling was that day's test for myself, making sure that I was alive. And on those days when my own philosophy wasn't enough to motivate me I would think of Gonzalez, my fellow wildland firefighter, and the phrase he often repeated anytime someone whinged or moaned about discomfort, he would say, "It builds character."

That "character," that muscular strength that I had built up paid off when it came time to fight fire. It was not that I was able to outwork my youthful cohorts because of my discipline, only that I was able to keep up with them, and barely at that.

Being physically strong for the job, staying fit, working hard, using my body as a beast of burden - these are things that I enjoyed about wildland firefighting. I enjoyed them because it was not long before that I had been robbed of brawn and sapped of vitality. I had come as close to death as I ever have, all because of one bastard mosquito bite, and the aforementioned Dengue Fever.

A year prior to my rookie fire season I had contracted Dengue Fever - which if you've never had it, I highly recommend NOT contracting it, if one can avoid doing so - a charmingly named tropical disease that has been known to take lives and whose symptoms include: rashes, vomiting, headaches, dehydration, joint pain, muscle pain, and, of course, fever. It lasted for ten days and in its wake I was left a fragile and shriveled husk. Though Dengue no longer plagued me its after affects lasted for many, many months. Get-up-and-go - gone. Physical strength - vanished. I found myself sleeping for ten to fourteen hours per day, not by choice. Thoughts alone would tire me out. It took four months to get my vitality back, six months to regain muscular strength, and one and a half years to regain the twelve pounds that I had lost during my ten-day fever.

Therefore, having lived through being the definition of weakness, I appreciated the pain and the struggle of fire seasons, every mile ran, every mountain hiked, every cut of the chainsaw, every fireline dug, every lungful of smoke, every ounce of sweat; it all reminded me that I was still alive.

Looking back, the way that I now perceive wildland firefighting is that it was a whetstone, and I, a dulled blade.

Cut to: fighting forest fires. The truth about wildland firefighting is that there are a hell of a lot of 'hurry up and wait' moments. Even in the busiest of fire seasons when trees and land are burning at hellish rates, at best, it's about a 70/30 split – 70% waiting to 30% fighting fire – and that is being generous, some fire seasons it can be more of a 90/10 ratio, or in really bad fire seasons (good for the public, but bad for the paychecks of wildland firefighters) a 95/5 split. Regardless of the ratio, the point is there was plenty of time to talk to your crewmates about everyone's favorite subject: themself. Which made the crew motto, "There are no secrets on the Highlands 20," even more relevant.

It was like having a captive audience of amateur

priests/psychotherapists with you for 24-hours a day for three months straight. We all confessed far too much about ourselves whether we wanted to or not, but that's what happens when there are no other distractions, you tend fill the void with yourself. You pondered. You questioned. You brooded. You cursed. You talked about your dreams, your goals, your loves, your desires; you talked about your past and your future. You never talked about the present – there was no need to: we were all there, living it together.

Over the course of my first fire season, through countless hours of free therapy/confessions, a pattern that I had never seen before was brought to my attention. In my past few failed relationships I had been the connective tissue – but it wasn't because of my faults, fears, or stubbornness that had destroyed them. I had started each relationship on solid ground, but as time passed I hadn't stood up for myself or related how I truly felt for the irrational fear of losing them if we were ever at odds. Each time I acquiesced to their wants and needs and of who they thought I should be. I did whatever I could to please them, never arguing or breeching subjects that would cause discomfort, and in doing so lost myself along the way; what emotional strength I had going into the relationships withered into weakness. And it was only through talking with my crewmates that I had that epiphany, making my time on the Highlands 20 that much more crucial for my own evolution.

On a hot August day in 2013, the kind where the sun burns a bright magenta through a smoke shroud and beats down upon men like a fever, I was mopping up on the Eagle Fire, side-by-side with Rich, a Highlands 20 crewmember, when he told me, “People will treat you the way you allow them to treat you.” Fireworks went off in my head. Jackpot lights flashed and bells and whistles rang loud and clear. Mind blown.

Wildland firefighting had done the unexpected. It acted as a mirror, that when held up to my face showed me where I had gone wrong in life, in love. It gave me the tools to heal, to overcome, to evolve; gave me the insight into being strong in all areas of my life. The howling beast within was finally set free. Who knew that being a crewmember of the Highlands 20 would prove to be beneficial to more than just my empty wallet? Who knew that fighting wildfire would be so transcending? Who knew that this midlife rite of passage, this time spent sweating and toiling in fire, and smoke, and soot would change the trajectory of my life, never to be the same again?

2018

It's all part of the Gig

The Highlands 20 hiking out of the Silver Star Fire (2013).
Photo Credit: Jeff Cedarbaum

It's funny how there are seasons in one's life that, though short in comparison, define the rest of their time on earth. I vividly recall, with all of my five senses working overtime, when wildland firefighting began for me, just as easily as I can put my finger precisely on the moment it ended, when my body was wracked with pain and sanity had unraveled itself until I had no more fucks to give, the part in the story where the hero realizes that he is no longer as invincible as he once was.

When I first joined the Highlands 20, once described as an elite 20-man hand crew, I was thirty-four, it was mid-summer in central Washington, and I stepped out of our squad's buggy and into the hot noonday sun ready to fight wildfire for the first time. The air smelled of timber smoke and acrid sweat and reverberating through the mountains was the chud-chud-chud-chudding of a rotor (helicopter) as it passed overhead. Around me: my crew, of which, I was one of twenty, the oldest by a decade or so, and all I could think of were the words that Larsen, my sawyer, had told me a month prior, "Once you pop your fire cherry, boy, that's it. You're addicted," and something within whispered that I would never be the same. In truth: I never was.

A few weeks later on the way to a fire, a song played in the buggy that went "It's better to feel pain than nothing at all," and late at night as I lay in my sleeping bag upon hard and rocky soil I wondered if that were true. I know now, as I knew then, that the song was speaking of matters of the heart, but in the moment, my feet were blistered, my knees felt as if they would give out on me at any second, and my back was stiff and knotted with aches. One of the positives of being a thirty-four year-old man and working and living with men a decade or so younger was the belief that like them, all conflicting evidence aside, I, too, was invincible.

*   *   *

I could have worked a different job, had the Fates seen fit to deal me a different hand, during a different season, and I, myself, were different. I could have worked on an oilrig or on a pot farm or even as a fast food worker, but since I am writing about my life, my experience, I am writing about wildland firefighting, which is the hand I was dealt.

That night of my first wildfire, the Rattlesnake Fire, I lay in the dirt after a sixteen hour shift on my feet, one side of me warmed by the campfire, the other cold and in the darkness, looking up at the night sky, amazed by the splash of sparkly stars spread velum-thin over the eternal blackness above, as around me my fellow wildland firefighters used their linepacks as pillows and curled themselves into the fetal position, Chester snoring louder than a hibernating dragon. For the next seven days we fought and eventually contained that fire.

Being in an alpha male/testosterone driven profession I often thought about how men my age did not take the career path I had chosen. I was also very aware that I was working harder than I had ever worked in my life. I was older and felt the job more in my bones and muscles than the rest.

That seven-day fire eased me into wildland firefighting. During those days of hiking and cutting and digging fireline I talked about my future, how I would teach English abroad and how I did not think I would ever fight fire again. How wrong I was. I was a wildland firefighter for a total of four fire seasons, four summers.

Looking back it seems to me that my first fire season was the most fulfilling, the most fun, the most life changing, and you'll perhaps understand that as I carry on. I want to reveal to you what it is like to be a wildland firefighter in your mid-30's, the way three months easily slides into four years and how the only difference you notice is more gray in your beard and a few more breaks in your heart. The mountains are engulfed in flames; I walk into Fire Camp at thirty-four, a rookie, and exit an older and wiser veteran. My goal in this essay is to clarify for you, and most importantly to myself, why I stopped fighting wildfire.

Wildland firefighting is thought of to be for the brave and the strong. There is more to it than that, at least for those of us who chose that career path after thirty-odd years of life under our belt: wild firefighting is a young man's game.

*　　*　　*

I remember the Eagle Creek Fire, one dark and windy August night on a mountaintop outside of Leavenworth, Washington. My fire crew, the Highlands 20, had battled the blaze up the criminally steep, sandy mountain, and was then, at 23:00, tasked with monitoring the fire throughout the night to make sure no embers jumped the fireline and started a spot fire below our position. That order came after an already brutal eighteen hours of wildland firefighting – hiking, cutting, digging. Exhausted. Beat. Whipped. We were all of those. Thankfully, our crewboss split us into groups of three. Gonzalez, Taylor, and I sat together in the black, the already burnt part of the forest. From our vantage, orange glowing knots illuminated the dark, remnants of the fierce blaze we had fought for dominance over. The wind picked up and the temperature dropped. The only source of heat came from the still smoldering duff of the forest floor, that, and body heat. We kept watch, or at least we tried to keep watch, but I know for a fact that the three of us fell asleep huddled together against the cold, the ashen forest floor warming us, coating us, becoming one with us.

Burnt over forests make sounds, not of animals or the rustling of pine needles - no, their sounds are those of destruction - the opposite of life. You don't hear the chirp of birds or squirrels frolicking instead you hear winds like high pitched curses screeching through the blackened branchless trees, followed by the squealing scream of those same blackened branchless trees as gravity claws at them, pulling them down until they crash with the sound of a falling giant being cut down at the ankles. Throughout the night I heard trees fall and land with a thunderclap, but I was too tired to move, too tired to give a damn if I lived or died.

At 7am, after a 26-hour shift, we hiked down the mountain to our buggies. As we loaded our gear and ourselves into our vehicles, all of us crusty from sweat, smoke, and ash, our teeth gritty with soot, I shed my Yellow, fire retardant shirt, which was a dingy grey at that point in the fire season, and chugged an entire ice cold Gatorade. Around me, water was downed in record time, cigarettes were lit, chewing tobacco was packed into lips and cheeks. For a brief moment the twenty of us sat beside our buggies, the sun cresting the mountains punching through the layers of smoke in shades of pink and red, each of us filthy, muted; the physical embodiment of a sigh. That's when Pat, 19, sandy haired, innocent, and a friend to all on the fire crew, turned his phone on and found out that his high school sweetheart had dumped him for another guy, a guy with a motorcycle, which, of course, meant that moments later we all knew, as there are no secrets on the Highlands 20. Before anyone could sympathize or break his balls, one of the squad bosses, clapped him on the shoulder, and said, "It's all part of the gig." Years would pass before I would come to understand the significance of that phrase.

*   *   *

It would be years because at that moment in time, honestly, I loved being a wildland firefighter. I loved the camaraderie, the bro culture – almost as if I had joined a fraternity - the laughter, the dirty jokes, the ball breaking, the lack of political correctness, the filthiness (in both body and mind). I loved the way I was treated by the community, the way random people from whatever town we were working outside of would shake my hand and thank me, and give me cookies, and pay for my laundry. I loved that the ladies loved that I was a wildland firefighter, that magic feeling of spending time with a beautiful woman post fire season after spending 90 days in an all-male-testosterone-fueled-environment, that first kiss, that first lay, nothing can compare. I loved that I did a job that everyone saw as ballsy and heroic.

Once, at a destination wedding in Mexico, I was sitting around a table of ten – strangers from Los Angeles – and each person began to introduce themself in the classic LA fashion; name quickly followed by job, in order to set the social pecking order. Around me: lawyers, accountants, production staff from CSI, and then there was me, the lone wildland firefighter. All eyes zeroed in on this kid. No one wanted to hear about pending lawsuits or talk of taxes or the new season of a syndicated television show, no, they wanted to hear all about wildland firefighting – something exotic and wild and unthinkable from the point of view of their caged urban minds. I wowed them with tales of blood, sweat, tears…and of shit. Yes, actual shit. Of which I am about to regale you with now.

*   *   *

My squadboss, flipped on the lights to the barracks and shouted, "Wake up, you motherfuckers!"

This was not the first time that I had been woken up in the middle of the night by an overhead to drink beer until daylight. My squadboss, however, did not want to drink beer. He wanted answers.

"Get the fuck out of bed, Squad One!" His face, red from rage and alcohol, his words on the brink of slurring, out of bed the eight of us stood stock-still – not saying a single word. He made his rounds getting in each of our faces – nose to nose – shouting obscenities, asking rhetorical questions, and making unbelievable statements. "You think you're crazy? Do you? Let me tell you, you're not. I've seen crazy," he yelled, pointing a finger at his twitching eyes, "I've seen blood!" He walked from member to stunned member of Squad One, and said things like, "Gonzalez, you're from California, you represent Rio Hondo Fire Academy and the United States Marine Corps! Hoorah! Why the fuck are you here again?" After confronting all of us, he then challenged us, all of us at once, to a contest of strength. "I know what you're thinking, you motherfuckers. You want to kick my ass," he then burp/yelled out the words, "bring it on!" As suddenly as the words had left his mouth, a wave of sobriety swept over him, re-judging the odds, he lost steam and sobered up enough to realize he was our squadboss and how utterly shitfaced he was and stumbled back out of the barracks, but before he left he shouted the one unanswered question that haunts me to this day, "I want to know who shit the g**damn dryer!"

*   *   *

But still, I loved being a wildland firefighter. I loved that wildland firefighting was everything that I thought that it would not be. Nothing was mundane; everything was exciting, dirty and drenched in sweat. There was always something unexpected, missions to be completed, mountains to be hiked, obstacles to be conquered, things I had never thought of, or even seen before.

I was once flown into a fire via helicopter, the raging flames beneath, the jarring chud-chud-chud-chudding of the rotor above my head, or the time I was boated out of a fire, how the cool spray of river water hit my face and made rivulets of mud across my cheeks, or my first backburn, a tactic used to eliminate fuel between wildland firefighters and the fire itself, where I used a drip torch to unleash my inner pyromaniac and helped set ablaze 1400 acres of timber, or all the unforgettable individuals I met along the way – Frenchie, who was one of the hardest working men I had ever seen and who's catch phrase, "Don't be a pussy," became a crew mantra, or the Cali Boys; three wildland firefighters who brought their SoCal swagger to the backwoods of Washington State, or Hambone, an artist type who packed a rubber pussy in his linepack, and on those rare nights we used tents, the sound of squishy rubber could be heard emanating from his.

*　　*　　*

I made plans for the end of every fire season and there seemed be an endless stream of days before each season's end. You see I could make all the plans for the future I wanted, and none of it mattered. I held a bizarre point of view as a wildland firefighter: it never dawned on me that I was in the real world doing that job. In my fevered brain it felt like a strange and feral dream and at the end of each fire season I would wake up and again restart my life in normal society. Far from the typical wife and kids routine the majority of men my age find themselves in, who need stability rather than adventure in their employment, I found myself working with men a decade or more younger, men without familial obligations. They appeared to be fighting fire for the same reason I was, each of us on a quest for cash-money, not caring what kind of hardships we had to endure to make that happen. "Fortune and glory," I used to say, quoting Indiana Jones. We were temporary expatriates from mainstream America who always knew how much overtime we had earned, or in my case, how many days were left on my contract.

*　　*　　*

Someone who lives for fire seasons lives with an apocalyptic mindset, even when the world is not on fire. I went on a spring break road trip, for example, and drove through the Sequoia, Redwood, and Yosemite National Parks, as my girlfriend gawked at the majesty of the mountains juxtaposed against the bluest skies in all of America, all I saw were those same mountains covered in hot-as-hell-orange flames, those same old royal trees burning angry. She saw Heaven. I saw Hell. That, however, is a lingering result of being a wildland firefighter.

* * *

I don't know if its possible for the public at large to completely grasp what wildland firefighting, the actual act of wildland firefighting as well as living as one, means to those of who have done it or still do it. To residents of rural America, those who live on farms, out in the woods and on one-lane gravel roads, where summertime is spent in preparation for winter, particularly those in the Western United States where fire seasons have become so prevalent in the past few decades that they are commonplace, to them: wildland firefighting is a plausible vocation. But for those who do not live in rural western America - those who have no concept of wildland firefighting and imagine all firefighters as riding around in massively elongated candy apple red fire engines, removing cats from trees, and rushing into flaming buildings with tanks of oxygen strapped to their backs, or posing shirtless for calendars with chiseled abs, iron bending biceps, and sparkling smiles - for those people firefighters are an archetype of heroism and strength, an unbelievably romanticized concept, the core of selflessness and integrity, the American hero incarnate. Wildland firefighting is just as heroic and selfless, only filthier, less sexy, and far more demanding.

*　　*　　*

I had never thought of becoming a wildland firefighter until the age of thirty-four; the notion had never crossed my mind. Truthfully, I found it hard to comprehend those young men for whom wildland firefighting was not simply a short-lived adventure but a viable career option, men who graduated from renowned wildland firefighting academies and had stacks of certificates and qualifications and a game plan for how they would climb the ranks of the firefighting world. I was not like that.

I purposefully never advanced as a wildland firefighter. I loved the work. I loved the brotherhood. I loved being told what my mission was and then going out and accomplishing it. However, I was never keen on being responsible for the lives of others. I had no desire to be a squadboss or crewboss. For me, it was a challenge - a way to test my mettle and make money - a means to an end, my goals lay elsewhere. As those around me spent hundreds of dollars on linepacks and sought volunteer employment as structure firefighters in the off-season, I plotted and planned and visualized my life outside of fire. Maybe it was the lines on my face, or the fact that my knees had given out on me a few times during my first fire season, but I could never commit myself to wildland firefighting as the others had.

All I ever did was to try to do my best. Well, most of the time I tried to do my best, but after weeks on end of fighting wildfire without proper time to recover one's physical and mental faculties, I lost my will to give a damn. This feeling of callousness came during my third fire season, the fire season of 2015. It was my third summer of wildland firefighting, at the age of thirty-six, when I first understood that I was not invincible, I had limits, that it did mean something and some things are permanent, all the smartass remarks, all the disagreements, all the pain felt in my body, every bit of it.

* * *

Wasn't it all supposed to be an adventure? A grand challenge to test myself and make money in the process? These days, when memories of my life as a wildland firefighter come to me, they rush in in dreamlike sequences. The vast majority of my time as a wildland firefighter was spent sweating profusely. I would sweat so much under my fire retardant Nomex that after a short while I ceased to notice my own funk. Now the slightest trace of soiled and aged body odor, a scent that would cause upheaval in the stomach's of most, triggers memories of wildfire. Neither can I smell the sickly sweet smell of bar oil or the pungent punch of chainsaw fuel, either is bad enough by itself but in combination they act as a time machine to the past, or the distinct types of smoke found in wildland firefighting. There are smells that are particular to different types of smoke, varying from the lung-chokingly-thick scent of burning timber, to the earthen odor of a grass fire, to the roasted soil scent of a root wad that's been smoldering for days. Smells are not the only purveyors of memory. Music also takes me back. The Lumineers. Motley Crue. Calvin Harris. Beastie Boys. Garth Brooks. Some classic rock tune that was popular in 1980 or 1981 that encouraged us to not stop believing years later in 2013.

I expect that a lot of wildland firefighters have the same fire porn on their computers at home – pictures of fire in all its burning and destructive and awe-inspiring glory. I recall sitting on the side of a mountain on the Clockum Tarps Fire outside of Wenatchee, Washington. The sun was gone. The moon was out. Fire operations had ceased for the day, which did not mean the fire itself was out, only that we had secured our Division and would be spiking out (prepared camping on the fireline). As we ate our dinner of MRE's (Meals Ready to Eat – packaged dehydrated food eaten by soldiers) we sat in silence, probably the only time we weren't breaking balls or talking shit. The silence was brought on by what we were witness to. From our perch we watched as the mountain that faced us lit off in furious oranges and devilish reds against the black backdrop of night, all the while, as each tree ignited and was consumed, all to be heard was the hellishly loud roar made by them like that of a hundred booming jet engines. When the fire had died down and our stale meals were finished, we retrieved our sleeping bags from our buggies and set up camp.

I remember standing by outside of those same buggies on that same fire for four solid days, standing by for the conditions to be spot-on-precise in order for us to do a backburn. We stood by for the winds to be in our favor, for the relative humidity to drop, for the PIG

(Probability of Ignition) to be 100%. We stood by for so long that when the time came and it was my turn to burn, I had to center myself and focus on lighting fire to acre upon acre of grass and timber rather than laugh at the days of dirty jokes that had been told in preparation for the burn. I loved to backburn, loved to feel the heat from the flames as they pushed me along, adrenaline moving my body up and down mountains, knowing that I had only two choices: keep going or be engulfed in flames.

Then there were the lone nights off we had, our R&R nights, the nights we had earned after fourteen days straight of fighting wildfire. Those were the nights that we stayed up all night drinking. It's extremely difficult to wrestle with zero sleep and a head full of booze as the sun is rising in the East, which was not why we stayed awake, but it seemed as good a time as any to let out our aggressions. The barracks would be cool and dark and I could sleep all day, but without fail, our R&R always ended with us heading out before sunrise to another fire. With a few hours of sleep and liquor on our breath we would pour ourselves into our buggies and be on the road before sunup. I could do my job on a few hours of sleep and a greasy diner breakfast in me, chugging water on the way to fires in order to sober up and keep myself from going down with dehydration later in the day.

*   *   *

I loved being a wildland firefighter, loved the order and controlled chaos of being on a fire, loved the systematic flow of getting orders from our crewboss, then breaking off into our separate squads and accomplishing that day's mission. And when our time on the fire was up, whether the fire was contained or we had timed out and had to leave, we could look at the divisions we had defended and know we had given our all and the proof was in swaths of land untouched by flame.

Despite my lack of speed I also loved hiking, loved humping up mountains, head down, eyes focused on the heels of the man in front of me, loved how I was able to unleash my mind and be in other places and other times while my body carried on.

From behind my sawyer I pulled branches and limbs and rough cut logs and burnt trees, anything he cut with the chainsaw; it did not matter the size, I was his swamper, and I pulled them away in order for him to have a clear cutting area, and when I could look back at the line we had made, separating the green, the unburnt area, from the flame front, and the diggers moving behind us in synch scraping down to bare earth, that made me indefinably happy. I was also darkly pleased when we would roll back into an ICP (Incident Command Post – a mobile base camp) in the violet summer dusk and see the new fire crews that had just arrived, fire crews with fresh faces wearing unsoiled Yellows, twinkles of hope in their eyes, as my crew stood in the chow line looking like we had cheated death another day, our faces and clothes crusted with ash and salted sweat, and on all of our minds: the delicious guarantee of a fat paycheck and summer adventure.

When the off-season came, I held onto that reverence for wildland firefighting. I glossed over the hardships and focused on the friendships, the laughter. I longed to be back on the fireline with a distinct purpose, a mission that I could focus solely on and not give a damn about the needs or wants of the world outside of wildfire.

I loved mopping up, which occurred after a fire had been contained, and crews would be tasked with roving through the burnt acreage checking the black (the burnt over area) for smokes or deceptively burning stump holes or smoldering ash pits. It gave us, the fire crew, a time to move slower and let our guard down just enough to have some fun, tell some stories, and, for me, to reflect on who I was and how I had gotten there. I remember one particular day in July of 2014 on the Carlton Complex in the Methow River Valley when we were mopping up. I was wearing a bladder bag, an extra 40lbs of weight on top of my 45lb linepack (think of it as the world's heaviest and most useless water gun, as it has a small brass wand that trickles the water out one puny stream at a time). I was on a seek and destroy mission, seeking out any hotspot and digging it up and mixing it with water, when I came across a patch of boiling dirt. Yes, dirt does boil if it gets hot enough. As I looked down, my eyes became unfocused and I saw not the bubbling earth at my feet but a vision of the girl I loved, the girl who had broken up with me the day before fire season began, the girl whose memory I had been trying to bury beneath a thousand smartass remarks and cans of cheap beer, and I began to cry. Good Lord, I could not let anyone see me cry. I was looked up to. I was a leader, of sorts. I had a reputation to uphold. Weakness was not tolerated in the Highlands 20. Composing myself, I smeared the tears into the dirt on my face and finished my mission, once again shoving those feelings of hurt and loss into the hole she had left in my heart. Yet I still loved wildland firefighting, because at the end of the day, the end of the season, it was something I could be proud of.

* * *

You may have guessed already that it took me three summers of fighting wildfire before its spell of wonderment wore off, before I understood the meaning in that phrase, said so long ago to the heartbroken Patty, which, for me, meant that even stopping being a wildland firefighter is all part of the gig.

* * *

I will tell you the exact moment that it became as clear as a crystal ball. I was thirty-six, days away from thirty-seven, and it was the last day of my third fire season at my end of season evaluation, sort of a parting powwow where my squadboss and crewboss would tell me how I fared throughout the fire season. I had reached my limit as a wildland firefighter and reached an impasse with my superiors, they chastised me for not taking on more and more responsibility and for not trying harder, when in fact that fire season I had given it my all and I did not want the responsibility they so craved to adorn me with. I could no longer hike up mountainsides for miles and miles without feeling a grinding pain in my hips. I no longer had any interest in hearing from my squadboss how we were a bunch of lazy bastards despite the fact that we had been running and gunning 95 out of a 100 days that fire season, and the human machine, or, at least, my human machine, was not built to run like that. I could no longer be bothered by the severity of perilous situations, as I had grown callous to the dangers of the job. I had seen too much wildfire and backburned so many times that my lust for it had changed to mediocre contempt.

They wanted me to change who I was and become who they thought I should be, as if it were as easy as downloading a program into my brain. But I could not. I would not. Not out of spite, but out of the principal of the thing. By that point they had known me for three fire seasons, knew who I was and what I brought to the table, knew my personality, my sense of humor, and that I was a decade or more older than the rest of the fire crew; therefore change in that respect was not an option. Again, as my crewboss and squadboss read me the riot act, scolding me more for whom I was than what I had done. I sat there taking it, knowing that this was my swansong, my cue to leave. When they had finished berating me they ended with this question. “If we were to hire you back next fire season what would change, how would you be different?”

I pondered their question, rolling over in my mind all they had scolded me for – not taking enough responsibility, laughing too often, speaking my mind to the public and not maintaining the robotic status quo – and I knew I had to be straight with them, just as they had been with me. "I'm not going to bullshit you," I said, doing my best to keep it together, keep it professional. "I respect you too much to bullshit you. If you hired me again nothing would change. I am who I am; it's too late in the game to change my core." I then stood, shook their hands and continued, "I want to thank you though, I want to thank you for helping me realize that this is the end of my time on the Highlands 20. You've helped me realized that I have limits, and right now I've reached mine." For a moment, they sat slack-jawed, the vacant looks on their faces told me that was not the answer they had expected, nor the answer they wanted, but had rather anticipated me to beg and plead for a chance to be on the fire crew and to make promises of change that I did not intend to keep. I then asked them not to take it personal, and left wildland firefighting.

Technically, I did work a final fourth fire season as part of a wildland fire engine crew, but as I only worked a total of five days out of 100 on active fires, I'm ashamed to lump myself in with the likes of initial attack crews, hotshots, or smokejumpers, and don't really count that summer.

It has been three years since I left the Highlands 20, and now I live in Saigon. Most of the men that I worked with, and are still close with, are not surprised by my moving here, as it was what I said I was going to do when I had finished my university degree, and I am a firm believer in setting and accomplishing goals. For those that are shocked I left the world of wildland firefighting behind for a classroom full of Vietnamese youths. I tell them how I wished I had started wildland firefighting when I was younger, and how they should enjoy these years that they are able to hike up ungodly steep terrain without the pain and slowed recovery time that comes with age.

Wildland firefighting is a young man's game, and though I feel young at heart, and am often thought of as a decade or more younger than I am, I benefit from the wisdom that my age affords me, and though it's all part of the gig, I now know my limits. In my heart I will always be a wildland firefighter, even though it seems so long ago that I was one.

2018

ABOUT THE AUTHOR

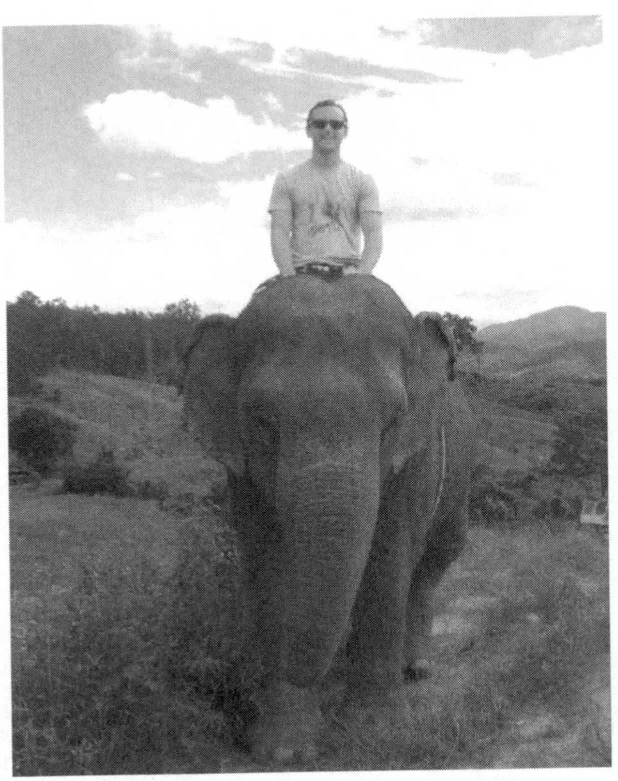

Charles R. Vaught Jr. was born in Texas in 1978. As well as being a wildland firefighter, he has worked as a commercial fisherman in Alaska, planted trees in the wilds of the Pacific Northwest, associate produced live events in Los Angeles, traveled through Asia for two years, earned a Bachelor's degree in Creative Writing from Eastern Washington University, and taught English in Vietnam. He is currently working on a book based on his time spent as a commercial fisherman

Find out more about Charles and his writing at: charlesvaught.com

Made in the
USA
Lexington, KY

55237806R00139